BRITISH PRIME MINISTERS IN 100 FACTS

CLIVE PEARSON

AMBERLEY

This book is dedicated to my family who have been so encouraging and supportive.

First published 2022

Amberley Publishing
The Hill, Stroud
Gloucestershire, GL5 4EP

www.amberley-books.com

British Library Cataloguing in Publication Data.
A catalogue record for this book is available from the British Library.

ISBN 978 1 3981 0965 0 (paperback)
ISBN 978 1 3981 0966 7 (ebook)

Typeset in 10pt on 12.5pt Sabon.
Typesetting by SJmagic DESIGN SERVICES, India.
Printed in the UK.

Contents

INTRODUCTION

In days of yore monarchs wielded enormous powers. Following the 'Divine Right of Kings' principle they could dispense with their feeble parliaments and only when so inclined did they rely on a 'chief minister'. However, with the passing of time monarchs became increasingly cash-strapped and had to beg their parliaments for greater grants and supply via taxation. Very soon, Parliament began to contest the need for these extra monies and even reject the requests. By the reign of Charles I (1629-1649) the issue of whether the king had divine autocratic powers or more limited ones was put to the test in a civil war (1642-1651). The king lost his head (figuratively and literally) and Parliament won a resounding victory, forcing monarchs thereafter to accept a more reduced role. After the 'Glorious Revolution' of 1688 Parliament further asserted its authority and William III and Mary were compelled to accept the terms offered them. Take it or leave it! It was a far cry from the absolute monarchies of medieval days. Eventually, the king or queen could only rule through and with the consent of Parliament and its 'chief minister' who commanded majority support there.

One of these ministers was Sir Robert Walpole who took up office in 1721 and became recognised as the first Prime Minister. It must be noted, as well, that as he served for nearly 21 years he is also the longest serving of all the 55 politicians that have reached that exalted position over the past 300 years. The shortest serving was the unfortunate George Canning, whose premiership lasted all of 119 days. Pitt the Younger at 24 was by far the youngest upon first crossing the threshold of No.10 Downing Street while Lord Palmerston (aged 70) was the oldest. Gladstone at 84 lays claim to being the oldest upon his retirement.

Of course, it goes without saying that the position of premier is whatever the holder wishes to make of it. It all depends on the character, temperament and abilities of the top man or woman. Some have been rather ineffectual or even just figureheads, such as Spencer Compton and the Duke of Devonshire in the eighteenth century. The Earl of Rosebery at the end of the nineteenth century was totally unsuited to the role and suffered a nervous collapse as a result. Others, on the other hand, have been able to wield great power and authority, such as Pitt the Younger, Gladstone and Winston Churchill. And yet such pre-eminence has always proved transitory. Margaret Thatcher is a case in point. She had appeared invincible during much of her time in office but in the end failed to work in a collegiate manner with her cabinet and further undermined her own position with the poll tax. Indeed, some unfortunate event or circumstance usually brings down those who had once seemed so high and mighty.

In reality, prime ministers do not have limitless powers. To begin with, they have always needed the support of Parliament and the cabinet. In addition, from the mid-nineteenth century onwards the party has proved a powerful restraining force. As the head of government, the prime minister must also deal with the media, which has often proved intractable. He or she may try to control it but cannot stop criticism. A final interesting point is that 10 Downing Street has been the official residence of all prime ministers throughout the last three centuries.

I do hope you enjoy the book.

1. WHIGS AND TORIES WERE THE TWO MAIN PARTIES

During the eighteenth and the early nineteenth centuries the two principal political parties were called Whigs and Tories. They were originally terms of abuse with Whig meaning 'horse thief' and Tory meaning 'papist outlaw'. The history of these names goes back to the time of the Stuart King Charles II and the years 1679-1681. The Tories supported the accession of his brother James II (a Catholic) as the rightful heir while the Whigs opposed it and wanted a Protestant claimant. In due course William III and Mary (James's daughter) came across from Holland and ousted James in the 'Glorious Revolution' of 1688-9.

Later the Whigs invited in the Protestant king of Hanover to become George I. However, supporters of James II and his descendants (the Jacobites) believed their man should be on the throne and twice, in 1715 and 1745, tried to overthrow the Georgian kings but without success. The bad news for the Tories was that they were too closely associated with the Jacobites and so both George I and George II understandably chose only Whig prime ministers. With the arrival of George III in 1760, Tories were once again back in favour and Pitt the Younger (1783-1806) can be seen as having created the basis of the modern Conservative, or Tory party. Incidentally, it is also the oldest political party in history.

We should not be under the illusion that these two parties in any way resembled modern ones. Throughout most of the eighteenth century they were very often loose groupings of noble families and wealthy commoners, and the distinctions were not always clear. Whigs were mostly aristocrats who supported limited reform and restricting the powers of monarchs, whereas Tories were generally country gentry against any religious toleration (despite supporting the Catholic Jacobites before) or foreign wars.

At election time parties in this period did not have national campaigns with a programme or manifesto. Most MPs were not bent on a career or the pursuit of a certain policy but saw it merely as their duty to support the king's ministers unless they were clearly failing. These were the 'king's men'. Interestingly, as a result of this no general election in the entire eighteenth century ever led directly to a change of government. The king selected a prime minister and it was then his task to convince the broad mass of MPs to support his policies.

Elections themselves were riddled with corruption, with wealthy landowners controlling a sizeable number of constituencies within their estates. These 'rotten boroughs' often had a tiny electorate, but each produced two MPs. Obviously, the local lord would choose his family and friends to fill these seats as vacancies arose. Although there were some 'boroughs' in the towns which had a much larger electorate with strongly contested elections, these did not affect the overwhelming preponderance of aristocrats in Parliament.

It was a system that kept the upper classes in power in perpetuity. Unsurprisingly, there was very little appetite for reforming the system.

2. WALPOLE WAS GRASPING AND CORRUPT BUT EFFECTIVE

When Robert Walpole came to power in April 1721 the term 'Prime Minister' was not used and it may have seemed to many at the time that he was just another in the long line of king's ministers who held the title of First Lord of the Treasury. However, his tenure of office extended for almost 21 years and he left a lasting legacy to all his successors.

Walpole was born in 1676 and came from a family of county squires based in North Norfolk who could trace their ancestry back over 400 years. His father's parliamentary seat awaited him at the young age of 24 and like his father, he entered the House of Commons as a Whig. He soon made a name for himself as an up-and-coming politician, so much so that within four years he was offered his first government post. Party members were impressed by his administrative abilities and debating skills, as well as his general bonhomie. Undoubtedly, all this helped Walpole to speedily ascend the 'greasy pole'.

German-speaking King George I, who addressed Walpole in Latin, also came to see him as a safe pair of hands and after 1714 he was offered a succession of lucrative government positions, including that of Paymaster General, which he exploited to the full. Even before he became prime minister his venal nature was evident, as he had by then amassed a fortune, making himself one of the richest men in England.

You may well ask how it was possible for Walpole to stay in in the top job for so long. It helped that George I preferred to pass his time in Hanover, but royal patronage could only get you so far in the fickle world of eighteenth-century politics. So he made sure of his support by what would be regarded today as corrupt practices. MPs were blatantly bought off to make sure they voted the 'right way' and he exercised control over the House of Lords through his contacts and the granting of places and pensions. His famous bon mot was 'All these men have their price.'

However, his moderate policies of security, stability and peace did draw widespread support. By avoiding foreign wars and making financial and economic improvements he was able to substantially reduce the national debt as well as land taxes. By 1730 his popularity had soared and the general public referred to him as 'the great man'.

The good times didn't last for ever, of course. The 1734 election went badly and later he began to lose support in royal circles with the death of Queen Caroline, wife of George II, his most ardent supporter. In the end his peace policy fell apart when he was forced into a badly conducted conflict with Spain in the 'War of Jenkin's Ear'. By 1741 he could barely muster a majority in the Commons and so he promptly resigned.

He may have been greedy and corrupt, but he did leave Britain in a better shape than when he had first taken office.

3. THE WALPOLE COLLECTION ENDED UP IN RUSSIA!

As mentioned above, Walpole had amassed a large fortune by creaming off money from his positions in government. The most coveted of these was Paymaster General to the Armed Forces and although Walpole was not alone in lining his pockets in this manner, he was notoriously adept at doing so. He also acquired further wealth through his two marriages, both of which gave him dowries of £20,000. In addition, he accrued money to himself through his investments, the most notable of which was in the South Sea Company. Famously, the company shares became massively overvalued and a collapse ensued. The result was that many punters lost heavily, but Walpole made a killing as he sold his holdings just when the valuations reached their peak. His fortune is estimated to have been in the region of £100,000, which would make him a multi-millionaire today.

Walpole was, however, a man of taste and discernment when it came to the fine arts. He personally oversaw the construction of Houghton Hall in Norfolk, designed in the Palladian style. With plenty of cash in the bank he then set about adorning his mansion with art works. He bought a large number of paintings from the Wharton family for £1500 and this collection included works by Rubens, Rembrandt and Anthony van Dyke. He also acquired a large number of Roman busts.

Unfortunately, his grandson, George Walpole, fell into debt and secretly sold the 205 items to Catherine the Great of Russia in 1779 for over £40,000. They can now be found in the Hermitage Museum in St Petersburg.

4. SPENCER COMPTON WAS A NONENTITY WITH NO TALENTS

The second prime minister following on from Sir Robert Walpole was something of a disappointment, to put it mildly. His background is rather shrouded in mystery and no biographies have been written about him. Little is known of his childhood, but we do know that he was first elected to Parliament in 1698, firstly as a Tory before switching to the Whigs. He was rated as a poor speaker but soon developed a thorough knowledge of parliamentary procedures and he became liked for his friendly manner.

By 1715 he had perhaps found his ideal job as Speaker of the House of Commons, a position which by all accounts he held with great dignity and distinction for 12 years. He may not have been much of an orator but he is famous for a put down when a member complained about several noisy interruptions and demanded the right to be heard. Compton replied, 'No, Sir. You have the right to speak, but the House have a right to judge whether they will hear you.'

In 1722 Walpole offered him the lucrative post of Paymaster-General on top of the Speaker's job. (It seems that in those days the Speaker's position did not require you to be neutral and neither did it preclude you from holding a government position as well.) Like Walpole himself, he took advantage of the position and stashed away as much as £100,000.

George I died in 1727 and his successor, George II, wanted Compton for the premiership and on the assumption of the throne instructed him to write his declaration to the Privy Council. Alas, his protégé missed his golden opportunity by admitting to Walpole that he was unequal to the task! Instead, Walpole himself drafted it and kept his position.

Despite Walpole conferring on him the title of Baron Wilmington, he constantly conspired against his benefactor but remained a loyal supporter of the king. When Walpole finally retired in 1741 His Majesty soon settled upon the Baron to take over.

Alas, he again failed to live up to expectations. Although he held the title of First Lord of the Treasury he was, in fact, no more than a figurehead. It may have been ill health (he was 69 and suffered from kidney stones) or just his general lack of vigour which left him so bereft of authority. His administration, which lasted from February 1742 to July 1743, achieved little. Apart from some minor acts, his government was dominated by the War of the Austrian Succession (1740-5). Wilmington died in office five days after George II's glorious victory at the Battle of Dettingen.

Few lamented his passing. He was described as a 'plodding heavy fellow' with 'no talents' who enjoyed the pleasures of life such as eating and 'debauchery'. Indeed, he never married and is reckoned to have had several illegitimate children.

He may have held the highest offices in the land, but he was 'the king's nonentity'.

5. HENRY PELHAM FORMED A 'BROAD-BOTTOMED' ADMINISTRATION

If Compton cannot be counted as one of the great prime ministers of the eighteenth century, then Henry Pelham can. In a way he was the heir to Walpole and can be considered his natural successor as he shared many of the abilities and aims of his mentor.

He was born in 1694 and came from a landed aristocratic family. His father produced a large brood of 11 children from two marriages. Henry was the second surviving son and was especially close to Thomas, his older brother, who was heir to the estate and later became Duke of Newcastle. In a remarkable and unique set of circumstances, both brothers would assume the highest office.

His background helped him as he came from a great Whig family who were staunch supporters of George I and fiercely anti-Jacobite. Indeed, young Henry actually took part in the battle of Preston in 1715. He was then helped into Parliament by his brother who was already established there, and it was his sibling who then went on to promote and encourage him in his career.

After entering Walpole's government in 1721, Henry struck up a friendship with the great man. Walpole was deeply impressed by his administrative talents and his ability to argue the government's case in the House of Commons. The feeling was mutual and one writer described Henry as 'strongly attached to Sir Robert Walpole, and more personally beloved by him than any man in England'. In 1730 Walpole appointed him Paymaster General, but to everybody's surprise he did not enrich himself as was the norm for his predecessors – including Walpole himself. Although Pelham was said to have lacked charisma, he did not lack courage or loyalty to his friends. On one famous occasion he defended Walpole from a hostile crowd. Upon drawing his sword he declared, 'Now gentlemen, who will be the first to fall?'

After the death of Wilmington, George I chose Pelham to take over as he preferred his premiers to be sitting in the Commons. This created tensions between the two brothers, although Newcastle did his best to hide his jealousy.

Pelham carefully formed a 'ministry of all the talents', which included both Whigs and Tories. It was dubbed 'the broad-bottomed ministry', an oblique reference to the Prime Minister's own ample posterior. Like Walpole, he was intent on maintaining peace and reducing taxes. He successfully organised the crushing of the Jacobite rebellion of 1745 and brought about the end of the War of the Austrian Succession with the peace treaty of Aix La Chapelle in 1748. His reduction of the national debt thereafter impressed the king. He was also responsible for adopting the modern Gregorian calendar that we have today. He suddenly died in office in March 1754 aged 59. He was Prime Minister for 10 years and 191 days.

He was not a reformer but goes down as one of the best premiers of the period.

6. THE DUKE OF NEWCASTLE WAS 'A POLITICAL MEDIOCRITY'

Thomas Pelham-Holles, the Duke of Newcastle, enjoyed enormous wealth as well as wielding influence and patronage. He was, however, made to wait in the wings while his younger brother (above) held the premiership. This must have been galling as he had promoted and nurtured his brother's career but had not expected to be overtaken by him. Despite the jealousy that resulted, he remained close to his brother and was grief-stricken by his death. Alas, he lamentably failed to emulate his more able sibling.

He was born in 1693 and as the eldest son of an aristocratic family, wealth and titles fell into Thomas's lap. He collected both his father's legacy and that of his uncle, the Duke of Newcastle, which gave him an annual salary of £32,000 (or about £6.5 million in today's terms). He also became a landowner in 11 counties, but despite this he remained endlessly in debt due to his wanton extravagance, excessive generosity and the inadequate management of his estate. By the end of his life his debts amounted to £114,000.

He entered the House of Lords aged just 21 in 1714 and soon made his mark. It was not just due to his wealth and Whig credentials but also his closeness to King George I and to Walpole, who appointed him Secretary of State (South) – there were two Foreign Secretaries in those days – in1721. By 1727 his power of patronage and his ability to fix appointments made him indispensable to any government. It could be for this reason that he remained Secretary of State (first South, then North) for an unbeaten record of 30 years from 1724 to 1754.

After the death of his brother in 1754 he was the natural successor as premier in March of that year. However, wary of strong rivals he appointed mediocre men to the top positions. His government soon found itself involved in the Seven Years' War, which went badly at first with the loss of Minorca to the French. Severe criticism, particularly from William Pitt (the Elder), followed and eventually Newcastle was forced to resign in November 1756.

Unlike his brother, Thomas had shown himself quite incapable of leadership and his administration was seen by many as a disaster. Nevertheless, no government could be formed without him and so once again he became Prime Minister in June 1757; but with Pitt directing the war and very much the senior partner. It has become known as the Pitt-Newcastle government with the latter a mere figurehead. Pitt then successfully guided Britain to a series of stunning victories in 1759. However, by 1762 the duo had fallen out and Pitt resigned in a huff, forcing Newcastle to step down for the final time.

He served in government for 46 years and was Prime Minister for seven years and 204 days. It was one of the longest political careers in history. He was nevertheless seen as pompous and lacking in charisma and one historian described his time in government as 'an exercise in political mediocrity'.

7. THE FOURTH DUKE OF DEVONSHIRE HAD A HIGH SENSE OF DUTY

William Cavendish was a charming and unambitious man who was a loyal supporter of the Hanoverian kings. Little is known of his youth, but he was born into one of the most distinguished Whig families in England. He became an MP in April 1741 but only remained there for ten years before moving up to the House of Lords, where he took the title of Baron Cavendish of Hardwicke. He already had the courtesy title of Marquis of Hartington, but he also took on his father's title and became the Fourth Duke of Devonshire in 1755. So you could say he was a triple title holder.

He served in government under both the Pelham brothers and particularly distinguished himself as Lord-Lieutenant of Ireland, a post he held for a couple of years (1755-6). Immediately upon his return from Ireland King George II asked Devonshire to form an administration after the collapse of the first Newcastle administration (November 1756). He was at first reluctant but eventually agreed and, as with Newcastle later, William Pitt was to be the driving force. As Secretary of State (South) he was in charge of facing down Britain's enemies in the Seven Years' War, leaving Devonshire a mere bystander. The government was soon dominated by the issue of Admiral Byng who was blamed for the capture of Minorca by the French. He was clearly scapegoated and his trial and later execution caused the government to fall.

The ministry only lasted 255 days, which rates as the shortest government of the eighteenth century. Devonshire died in 1764 at the age of just 44.

8. THE THIRD EARL OF BUTE WAS TUTOR TO THE KING

John Stuart, 3rd Earl of Bute was the first Scotsman to take on the premiership but also the first Tory. Unusually, his rise to the top was almost entirely due to his closeness to the royal family and in particular to the future George III.

John was born in 1713 and was well educated, having studied at Eton and the University of Leiden. After this, he returned to his ancestral home on the Isle of Bute where he devoted himself to the study of botany and became an authority on British plants, as well as producing five sons and six daughters.

Upon a visit to London in 1747 he had a chance meeting with Frederick, Prince of Wales, at a race meeting. They got on like a house on fire and soon Bute was on extremely friendly terms with the prince's family. Frederick died in 1751 but his wife Princess Augusta, who remained very close to Bute, asked him to tutor their wayward son.

The sullen and lazy prince responded well to the new tutor and soon came to see him as a 'father figure' and in letters addressed him as 'My dearest Friend'. Bute gave him a very thorough all-round education but also imbued him with his own deeply held Tory prejudices, which painted the previous Whig ministries as corrupt and spendthrift.

In October 1760 the old king passed away and it was immediately clear to all that Bute was the power behind the throne of the new king, George III. Within a few months of his accession Bute was brashly inserted into the Whig government and made Secretary of State (North) in March 1761. He immediately created dissension over the direction of the war against France, causing William Pitt to depart the government. Bute himself took over the running of the war, resulting in another series of victories and in May of the same year he became Prime Minister. By February 1763 France and Spain sued for terms and in the Treaty of Paris Britain gained Canada, Florida and control of India.

One would be entitled to think that Bute would now be feted as a hero, but the opposite was the case. William Pitt fiercely criticised the treaty and Bute was heavily lampooned and pilloried in the press. There was ferocious prejudice against him as a Scot and the London mob came out against him (also for putting a tax on cider). Fearing for his life, Bute resigned. His ministry had lasted 317 days.

Bute left some important legacies. He arranged for Dr Samuel Johnson to have a pension of £300 a year to continue working on his dictionary and helped Princess Augusta to establish Kew Gardens. A species of tree is named after him, *Butea superba*.

After losing office he retired to his estates and wrote a nine-volume book on botany. He died in 1792. He was unfairly maligned at the time but history now records him as a 'responsible, cautious minister'.

9. GEORGE GRENVILLE HUMILIATES THE KING!

George Grenville was a skilled 'parliament man' who maintained a high level of efficiency and administration. However, once he reached the highest office his major failing was his inability to remain on good terms with George III.

Grenville was born in October 1712 to an ancient Norman family. He was educated at Eton and Oxford before going on to follow a legal career. As the second eldest son he was always strapped for cash and this led him to be rather thrifty both privately and with the nation's finances.

He entered Parliament in 1741 and his career was helped along by his brother, Lord Temple, and his brother-in-law, William Pitt. Grenville was soon recognised for his qualities as a debater and in 1744 was made Lord of the Treasury before becoming Treasurer of the Navy ten years later. However, his breakthrough came with the premiership of Bute, who much admired him, and so he was made Leader of the House of Commons. Two years later he became Secretary of State (North) but this only lasted a short while before Bute stepped down.

Grenville was taken by surprise when offered the top job in April 1763, but his joy was somewhat short-lived when he realised that many of the top positions were Bute's appointees. It was clear that the king continued to rely on his old tutor. After four months Grenville confronted the king, who humbly agreed to consult only with his prime minister and no one else.

A notable event of Grenville's administration was the introduction of the Stamp Act in 1765. The government deemed it appropriate that the American colonies should help pay for the cost of the Seven Years' War and the stationing of troops there. The colonists would henceforth pay a tax on legal documents as well as newspapers and pamphlets. The reaction against this in America was ferocious and unexpected, as the tax seemed moderate. Grenville had unwittingly stoked the fires that would lead to the American War of Independence: the cry went up 'No taxation without representation'. The next government hastily repealed it.

Unfortunately for the prime minister, relations remained strained with the monarch. The king complained that he found the premier 'tiresome ... When he has wearied me for two hours, he looks at his watch to see if he may not tire me for an hour more.' He wanted to rid himself of this troublesome minister, but Grenville had Parliament's full support. It was now that Grenville overstepped himself. He demanded that the king sever all contact with Bute and his brother, James Stuart-Mackenzie. The king finally agreed but felt deeply humiliated and Grenville's triumph was not long lasting. The king searched desperately for a replacement and eventually came up with the Second Marquis of Rockingham in July 1765.

Grenville's government had only lasted for two years and 85 days and could have lasted much longer but for his lack of tact. He had, however, set new standards of ministerial efficiency and had an 'application undissipated and unwearied...'

10. ROCKINGHAM WAS A FOUNDER MEMBER OF THE JOCKEY CLUB

The Second Marquis of Rockingham was a man of great integrity but of modest abilities. He has generally been overlooked by historians but during his time in and out of office he created what came to be seen as the first principled reforming party. He was also a keen member of the racing fraternity.

Rockingham was born into a family of immense wealth in May 1730. He was educated at Westminster School and Eton before moving on to Geneva. He then went on the Grand Tour of Europe so popular at the time. Alas, he contracted a problem 'in his urogenital system' in Italy which plagued him throughout the rest of his life. At the tender age of 20 he unexpectedly became heir to his father's estate, which included the family home of Wentworth Woodhouse, near Rotherham, a vast palace containing 240 rooms.

To begin with, the new marquis devoted himself to his vast holdings, which included large parts of Yorkshire. He also started an interest in horse racing that led him to become a prime mover in the Jockey Club. He owned a string of winning horses, one of which (Whistlejacket), was painted by George Stubbs.

In the House of Lords he was a staunch supporter of the Whigs and George II. However, with the accession of George III his attitude changed. He was outraged by the new king inserting Bute, a Tory, into government and by the subsequent cull of leading Whigs. The Marquis soon developed into a major opposition figure who told the king to his face his disapproval of his actions.

Surprisingly, the king, desperate to replace Grenville who had so humiliated him, selected Rockingham in July 1765. The new premier had had no previous ministerial experience (only three other premiers have had this dubious honour – Ramsay MacDonald, Tony Blair and David Cameron) and his government was dominated by his racing friends. Despite this, the government took one important step, the repeal of the Stamp Act that had so infuriated the American colonists. The hostility of William Pitt led his government to fall after just over a year. For the next 16 years the Marquis stayed in opposition forming the 'Rockingham Whigs', who held strictly to policy and principles. They were very much guided by Edmund Burke, a notable political theoretician, who believed that George III was exceeding his constitutional powers as set out in the 'Glorious Revolution' of 1688 when William III and Mary had accepted their reduced rights as monarchs.

Rockingham started his second administration in March 1782 and he declared it would be one of reform. He immediately rushed through three acts of parliament which swept away the king's usage of patronage and bribery, and markedly reduced corruption. Negotiations were ongoing regarding ending the American War of Independence when he died of pneumonia. He was 52 and had been prime minister for only one year and 113 days. For the time, his ideas were progressive and he left a strong Whig party.

11. PITT THE ELDER WAS A GREAT ORATOR AND WAR LEADER

William Pitt the Elder has gone down in history as the epitome of a great war leader, but he possessed an imperious nature with a ferocious temper. One commentator noted that he had 'the despotic nature of a tyrant'. He also spent a large part of his life suffering debilitating illnesses.

He was born in 1708 into a gentry background rather than an aristocratic one. However, his family became wealthy through trading in India and this allowed him an excellent education, firstly at Eton and then at the universities of Oxford and Utrecht. After returning home he managed to get a commission with the King's Own Regiment of Horse where, according to his letters, he ended up drinking heavily and whoring.

After the usual Grand Tour of Europe his brother offered him the 'rotten borough' seat of Old Sarum – which had an electorate of five! Not unexpectedly, he was returned unopposed and entered Parliament in February 1735.

Pitt immediately set himself up as a dissident Whig against the Walpole government and over the next few years he emerged as the most effective opposition speaker. His speeches were soon seen as a great occasion in which he painted himself as a 'patriot' whose sole aim in life was the prestige and power of Britain. He castigated successive governments in their handling of the War of the Austrian Succession, demanding a 'maritime strategy', as opposed to a continental one, with 'easy pickings' in the Caribbean and North America. His oratory brought him great popularity 'out of doors' with the public but few friends in top circles.

Pitt was anxious to get a position in government, so he tempered his criticisms and in 1746 he was offered the position of Paymaster-General in the Pelham government. His admirers saw this as a betrayal of his previous patriotic stance. Nevertheless, he held this position for nine years and proved a capable and incorruptible minister.

By 1755 Britain was sliding into another conflict, the Seven Years War. Pitt criticised its handling by the Newcastle government and was summarily dismissed. However, he returned to government with the Duke of Devonshire as premier in November. Pitt was appointed Secretary of State (South) and leader of the House of Commons, and he set about directing the war with tremendous vigour. He stated with a touch of arrogance, 'I am sure that I can save the country and nobody else can.' Although this government fell, he was reappointed under Newcastle and continued to direct the war on a world-wide scale. The years 1757 (Battles of Quebec and Plassey) and 1758 saw a series of successes but it was 1759 which marked the *annus mirabilis* or 'Year of Victories', which is perhaps unequalled in British military history. France was ousted from Canada and India and lost territories in the Caribbean and West Africa. The bells rang out continuously, but arguments later developed inside government over strategy and Pitt suddenly resigned in October 1761.

This, however, was not the end of his political career...

12. ...BUT A DISASTROUS PRIME MINISTER

After leaving the Newcastle government Pitt retreated to his family home. He had married at the ripe old age of 46 in 1754 and sired five children, three sons and two daughters. He particularly doted on his second son, also called William. He fostered in him a passion for politics and oratory and, as we shall see, his son developed into an even greater politician than himself.

Pitt returned to the House of Commons to denounce the Treaty of Paris of 1763, which finally ended the Seven Years' War. In what became a familiar scene he spoke for over three hours, gout-ridden and swathed in white flannel. He rather unfairly launched a scathing attack on the Bute government for being too lenient on France and Spain when, in fact, the terms were rather harsh.

Over the next few years Pitt became an increasingly difficult person to work with. He quarrelled with his close relations in Parliament and to his colleagues he came across as rather irritable and self-centred. In addition, his constant illnesses and bouts of depression left him an infrequent visitor to Parliament.

In April 1766 King George III unexpectedly summoned Pitt and asked him to form a government. It seems the king liked the tone of his recent speeches. It was now that Pitt made two unfortunate decisions which were no doubt the result of ill health. Firstly, he appointed himself Lord Privy Seal. In other words, he held no ministerial position including that of First Lord of the Treasury which normally accompanied that of prime minister. Secondly, he chose to move upstairs to the House of Lords and became the Earl of Chatham. Immediately he lost his reputation as the 'great commoner', the patriot and man of the people. He was quite unable to properly control his administration from the upper house and it soon became evident that he was a poor man manager, all too often behaving in an autocratic way with his cabinet.

Surprisingly, he had no clear objectives for his government and due to gout and a deep depression he became an increasingly infrequent visitor. The unfortunate Revenue Act, passed in his absence, placed customs duties on tea in America, which led to the famous 'Boston Tea Party' in 1773. From January 1767 onwards, Chatham spiralled down into a nervous breakdown, but it was not until February 1768 that the king finally accepted his resignation.

A year later he had fully recovered but never returned to government. Alas, his gout did return and when he made a final dramatic speech against American independence in April 1778 he was once more swathed in flannel. At the end he stood up to make an intervention but collapsed in a fit. He died a month later. He was Prime Minister for two years and 76 days.

He had been an inspiring war leader, but ill health had prevented him from making a success of the highest office.

13. THE THIRD DUKE OF GRAFTON TOOK AFTER HIS ROYAL ANCESTOR

Augustus Henry Grafton, 3rd Duke of Grafton, saw the business of government as irksome but necessary to one's station in life. He patently lacked the leadership skills and application to make for a successful political career.

He was born in September 1735 and was the great-great-grandson of King Charles II and his mistress Barbara Villiers. He was schooled in Westminster and Peterhouse, Cambridge. In 1757, at the age of 21, he was elected to Parliament but shortly after went to the House of Lords on the death of his grandfather and became the Third Duke of Grafton.

To begin with, he busied himself with his new estates as well as hunting and racing. Like his famous forebear he also liked to luxuriate in the pleasures of the flesh. Later on, despite having a wife and three children, he ostentatiously paraded his mistress, Nancy Parsons, who was a great beauty and was painted by Joshua Reynolds. This conduct drew disapproval in society. He later ditched Nancy, remarried and had another thirteen children!

After 1762 he turned to politics and was seen as a good debater. As a result he was offered the position of Secretary of State (North) in Rockingham's government and became the effective leader of the House of Lords. Later he was persuaded to be First Lord of the Treasury in Pitt the Elder's administration. However, this became an increasingly trying position. The ailing Pitt retreated to his country residence and for several months Grafton was reduced to being a messenger boy for the great man. Eventually, Pitt descended into a deep depression and Grafton was left to run the ship. Alas, Grafton lacked the authority and interest to direct the government competently. A former premier (George Grenville) described how one cabinet meeting was postponed for a race meeting at Newmarket.

Despite this, he formally became Prime Minister in October 1768 upon Pitt's resignation. The great issue of the day was the Wilkes case. John Wilkes was a radical MP who faced charges of sedition and expulsion from the House of Commons. Grafton favoured conciliation but was overruled by his colleagues. Likewise, he favoured repealing the duties on tea that so enraged the American colonists but was outvoted in cabinet.

When Pitt returned to Parliament in July 1769, he set about undermining the government. His supporters soon resigned their ministerial posts and Grafton was forced to leave office in January 1770. His administration had lasted one year and 106 days. At 33 he was to be the youngest Prime Minister after Pitt the Younger.

Afterwards, he held the post of Lord Privy Seal, but he really preferred to devote himself to his other interests which, rather surprisingly, included theology and the Unitarian Church. He died in 1811.

He was a dilettante who was bored by business and preferred 'sport and pleasure'.Grafton was certainly no grafter!

14. LORD NORTH WAS THE MAN WHO LOST THE AMERICAN COLONIES

Lord North has gone down as the worst prime minister in history as it was on his watch that the American colonies won their independence from Britain. However, as we have already seen, this is rather unfair as there are many others better qualified to wear that dubious badge of honour.

Frederick North, later styled Lord North, was born in April 1732. The Prince of Wales (father to George III) was his godfather – but may have been more than this! His Royal Highness had a reputation as a libertine and so may have been his actual father. Indeed, examination of portraiture suggests that North bore a much closer resemblance to the prince that to his supposed father.

Frederick attended Eton and Oxford and by all accounts was an exemplary student. This was followed by the usual Grand Tour of Europe, which lasted for three years. He then entered the Commons in 1754 as a Whig but was more Tory in his outlook. It was three years before he decided to make his maiden speech, which immediately impressed all observers. As a result of his debating skills he was soon offered the position of Lord of the Treasury and eventually he became Chancellor of the Exchequer and Leader of the Commons in 1767.

North's administrative abilities and command of the House led to his appointment as Prime Minister in January 1770. The first four years went well. War was avoided with Spain and he was able to reduce government debt of £140 million by £10 million, saving the exchequer £500,000 a year in interest payments. He was extremely assiduous and greeted all and sundry with wit and good humour.

Unfortunately, trouble was brewing. The government had wanted the American colonists to pay towards the cost of maintaining a British army in their defence. From the beginning both North and the king had sought to punish rather that conciliate the Americans. The government's stamp duty and the tax on tea had antagonised the Americans and had resulted in the 'Boston Tea Party' in 1773. North's response was the 'Intolerable Acts', which attempted to rein in the rebels but further embittered them. The First Continental Congress soon followed.

Initial skirmishes in the war began at Lexington in 1775 and within a year the colonists declared independence. At first the conflict seemed to be going Britain's way, but after two years she found herself on the back foot with General Howe's surrender at Saratoga. France, Spain and the Netherlands later joined the Americans and with the defeat of Cornwallis at Yorktown in 1781 it was clear the war was lost. 'Oh God, it's all over,' declared North on hearing the news and he resigned soon afterwards. In 1783 he returned in the short-lived Fox-North coalition under the Duke of Portland. He died of dropsy in 1792.

His premiership had lasted 12 years and 58 days. He had been a highly competent minister but not a war leader.

15. THE SECOND EARL OF SHELBURNE WAS 'THE GREAT OUTSIDER'

William Petty, the 2nd Earl of Shelburne was perhaps one of the cleverest people ever to have held the position of premier. He was admired for his intellect and progressive thinking but partly due to his character, failed to win over many friends in Westminster. As a result, his career can be seen as something of a disappointment.

He was born in Dublin in May 1737 to a pedigree Irish family who had dominated County Kerry since the twelfth century. Although his schooling was rather patchy, he was packed off to Oxford University but never took a degree. After this he decided to join the army. There followed a distinguished career in which he saw action in the battles of Minden and Kloster Kampfen in the Seven Years' War. He was decorated for bravery, received promotion to colonel and was appointed as aide-de-camp to King George III. Eventually, he would receive promotion to general.

While still on duty in Germany he was elected as a Whig MP in 1761 but failed to take up his place, as in the same year his father died. He was immediately catapulted into the House of Lords and overnight had become one of the richest men in England.

Shelburne was soon offered a position in government in the Board of Trade under Grenville in 1763. It was not a happy experience. Although he was a capable minister, he ruffled the feathers of those around him. He had annoyed the king and his colleagues saw him as touchy, arrogant and secretive about his decision making. After only four months in office, he resigned rather petulantly.

In opposition he became a devoted acolyte of Pitt the Elder and when the latter formed his administration in July 1766 Shelburne was offered the position of Secretary of State (South). Once again, he was often at loggerheads with those in the cabinet as he espoused more liberal, conciliatory policies regarding the American colonists and the problems of

Ireland. When Pitt finally threw in the towel in October 1768, he resigned along with him.

After this he settled into 13 years of opposition. However, he was not idle as he devoted much of the time to radical ideas with such thinkers as Jeremy Bentham and Samuel Johnson. One progressive proposal was that America should be given dominion status.

After serving briefly under Rockingham as Home Secretary, the king asked him to form a government in July 1782. As premier he negotiated peace terms with America and her allies, but divisions inside his cabinet and in Parliament over the peace settlement led to a lost vote of confidence and he resigned in March 1783. His old problems of man-management and an inability to build support had resulted in his downfall.

His premiership had lasted just 266 days. He died in in May 1803 aged 68. His career can be seen as a failure, but his ideas were ahead of their time.

16. THE THIRD DUKE OF PORTLAND WAS 'WORSE THAN USELESS'

William Cavendish-Bentinck, later the 3rd Duke of Portland, was a rather easy-going chap who was a great conciliator rather than a leader of men. His two short-lived administrations were separated by 25 years and in both of these he was very much a passenger. He has a further distinction in that in the first government he was a Whig but by the time he reached the second he had morphed into a Tory.

William was born in April 1738. His great grandfather, the first Duke, had come over to England from Holland with William III in 1689 and had had titles and land heaped upon him. The Third Duke was educated at Westminster School and Oxford. He then went off on his Grand Tour where he spent his time philandering and accumulating debts. In 1761 he was elected to Parliament but within a year his father died and he was transferred to the House of Lords. Portland's title and wealth soon led to his becoming a leading Whig.

His first experience of government was a minor post under Rockingham in 1765 and he stayed close to him until his demise. Afterwards, due to his conciliatory nature, Portland was seen as the best compromise candidate to head an administration dominated by Charles James Fox and Lord North. So in April 1783 he became Prime Minister in what has become known in history as the Fox-North Coalition. During his period in office, he signed the Peace of Paris which finally put an end to the American War of Independence. His government became unstuck, however, over the India Bill. This Bill was designed to restrict the authority of the East India Company and to give powers of patronage to parliamentary commissioners. King George III was determined to block this in the House of Lords and 'unconstitutionally' advised members that he wanted them to vote it down. Portland did little to defend the Bill, which was duly defeated and immediately the government fell. It had lasted 260 days.

After the French Revolution in 1789 he was persuaded to join Pitt the Younger's Tory administration. He became Home

Secretary in July 1794 and was notorious for his hard-line actions, bringing in repressive legislation against radical or revolutionary groups. He also showed scant concern for those suffering food shortages.

After Pitt died in 1806, Portland became a leading Pittite and the king asked him to form a government once again, in March 1807, despite his reluctance. Suffering from ill health he rarely attended cabinet meetings or Parliament and gave almost no direction to a talented but fractious cabinet. Unsurprisingly, the war against Napoleon went badly and two ministers even fought a duel. After suffering an apoplectic fit, he decided to step down. His second administration had lasted two years and 187 days.

It is little wonder that one historian described him as 'worse than useless'. Overall, this may be unfair, but he seldom rose above second rate in his career. He died in October 1809 leaving eye-watering debts of £500,000.

17. PITT THE YOUNGER WAS A REMARKABLE PRODIGY

William Pitt the Younger is the youngest prime minister on record by quite a margin, reaching the highest office at just 24 years of age. He was also the second longest serving at nearly 19 years. Pitt was also unusual for the time as he put selfless devotion to his country above personal interest. However, all this does not necessarily make him one of the very greatest premiers, as we shall see.

He was born in May 1759 and was the second son of the outstanding war leader William Pitt the Elder. He was selected by his father to carry forward the mantle of his political beliefs. With this in mind young William was hot-housed at home, being taught the classics as well as mathematics. Furthermore, his father personally coached him from a young age in the skills of oratory making him conduct simultaneous translations of Greek and Latin at sight. In this way the young Pitt was invariably able to find precise wording when speaking publicly. Very quick to learn, he entered Cambridge at the age of 14 and emerged with a Master of Arts at 17.

The young Pitt witnessed his father's last dramatic speech to the house on April 7 1778 when he eventually collapsed (12). Afterwards, William helped to carry him out of the chamber. It was not long before he himself entered Parliament in January 1781. His maiden speech came a month later and his powers of rhetoric riveted MPs and immediately marked him out for high office.

That opportunity came within a year when he was offered the post of Chancellor of the Exchequer under Shelburne. He made various changes and reforms that impressed observers. However, he resigned with Shelburne after only eight months in the post. Pitt in opposition later worked with the king to defeat the East India Company Bill as it was put to the vote in the House of Lords. This 'unconstitutional' move brought down the Fox-North coalition and the king immediately asked for Pitt, despite his youth, to form a government in December 1783.

To begin with this appointment caused some merriment, as it did when portrayed in *Blackadder the Third*:

> Pitt the Younger: 'I intend to put my own brother up as a candidate against you.'

> Blackadder: 'And which Pitt would this be? Pitt the Toddler? Pitt the Embryo? Pitt the Glint in the Milkman's Eye?'

The new prime minister lacked a majority. However, within a few months he called an election which secured his position. His main aims were to revive national confidence and to restore the economy. In both of these he soon proved adept by cutting out waste, setting up annual budgets and a sinking fund in order to pay off the national debt. His biggest headache was the Regency Crisis in 1788-9. King George III had his first bout of madness leading to the fear that the Prince of Wales would take over and install Charles James Fox (a Whig) as premier. At the last moment the king recovered and so the danger was narrowly averted.

So far everybody had been impressed with his command of the House and the economy...but the drums of war were sounding.

18. HE SACRIFICED HIMSELF FOR HIS COUNTRY

Prior to the French Revolution of 1789 Pitt had striven to maintain peace on the Continent through a 'concert of Europe'. He hoped that by bringing together the major players all serious disputes could be settled without resorting to war. This plan sadly failed to come to fruition, but it was ahead of its time. When war came, he was to be sorely tested.

At first Pitt welcomed events in France as Britain's traditional enemy in Europe was seriously weakened and the French people were seen to be liberating themselves from their autocratic monarchy. However, France's revolutionary armies were soon at war with their neighbours and spreading ideas which were considered dangerous for the aristocracy at home. Matters came to a head (!) with the execution of Louis XVI in 1792 and within a year Britain found itself at war.

Pitt's strategy was pretty much the same as his father's. Britain's navy would overrun French possessions overseas and at the same time the government would provide subsidies for coalitions of France's enemies (Austria, Prussia and Russia). However, by 1801 the results were disappointing. French Caribbean islands had proven difficult to hold and two continental coalitions had been decisively defeated.

At home, Pitt worked tirelessly to provide financial support for the war and in 1798 he felt compelled to introduce income tax for the first time. Amid mounting debt and food shortages he hastened to introduce legislation to crack down on various radical groups, some of which shared French revolutionary ideas. *Habeas corpus* was suspended and repressive legislation was brought in. Over 10 year there were 200 prosecutions, although many ended in acquittals.

It was clear by this time that Pitt's massive workload and his lifestyle were undermining his health. An argument with the king over the emancipation of Catholics linked to the union of British and Irish parliaments in 1801 led him to resign unexpectedly. Whether the two factors were linked is unclear, but his ally Henry Addington took over until Pitt's return in May 1804.

By now it was clear to many that Pitt's health was failing and events did not help. He exhausted himself in creating a third coalition, which was heavily defeated by Napoleon at Ulm and then Austerlitz in December 1805. He allegedly commented rather prophetically, 'Roll up that map; it will not be needed these ten years.' The only solace was Nelson's victory over the French and Spanish fleets at Trafalgar just prior to this. The French victory, however, was a hammer blow from which he would never recover. A month after this, in January 1806, he passed away, probably of a peptic ulcer. He had given himself over unstintingly to public service and had died in the process.

Although he had been remarkable as prime minister, there were many disappointments. He had espoused and spoken eloquently on such great causes as parliamentary reform, abolition of the slave trade and Catholic emancipation but had not implemented any of them. In addition, in war he had failed to emulate his esteemed father.

19. THE PRIME MINISTER WAS A 'THREE BOTTLE MAN'

In his youth Pitt the Younger had often suffered from poor health. His father's doctor, Anthony Addington, father of the future prime minister Henry Addington, had recommended that the young man could strengthen his constitution by regular horse riding and a liberal quantity of port wine every evening. Pitt adhered to this regime for the rest of his life and it is reckoned he downed as much as three bottles of the stuff a day. Although bottles had a smaller capacity in those days, recent estimates put this at one and two-thirds of a bottle in today's terms. This was a considerable amount and no doubt by the end of his life he verged on being an alcoholic.

William Pitt was generally quite shy and reserved in public but amongst his small group of close male friends he was known to be great fun and extremely witty. In his twenties neighbours were said to complain about his raucous antics going on well into the early hours. He could also be surprisingly playful even when in the highest office. One day with a few of his companions Pitt got involved in a pillow (or rather cushion) fight. They succeeded in partly blackening his face with some burnt cork but were interrupted by a visit of two lordships. He quickly cleaned up – but after the interview hostilities immediately resumed.

Although he had little female companionship, from time to time he had ladies to act as hostesses at his residences. For a while Jane, Duchess of Gordon did the honours (also in her own home) and later on his niece, Lady Nester Stanhope, took over. When after many years they met again, she enquired: 'Well, Mr Pitt do you talk as much nonsense now as you used to when you lived with me?' He replied, 'I do not know madam, whether I talk so much nonsense, I certainly do not *hear* so much.'

It was generally recognised by friends that Pitt was not a rounded person as he took almost no interest in music, art, theatre or literature. He was certainly not familiar with delicate matters relating to the opposite sex. In 1796 he developed a close friendship with the family of Lord Auckland and in particular with the daughter, Lady Eleanor Eden. The father was very keen that they should make a match and even the press expected a positive outcome. However, Pitt sent Auckland a long letter explaining that 'decisive and insurmountable' obstacles prevented a marriage. The meaning of this remains unclear.

Pitt's exhausting governmental responsibilities, his irregular lifestyle and his alcoholic intake took a toll. His doctor, Sir Walter Farquhar, and his close friends begged him to step down, but he remained obdurate. Towards the end all were shocked by his feeble and emaciated appearance. Farquhar commented that 'Pitt died of old age at forty-six as much as if he had been ninety.'

20. HENRY ADDINGTON WAS OVERSHADOWED BY HIS FRIEND

Henry Addington, the First Viscount Sidmouth, was a decent, honourable man who proved competent as prime minister. However, his time in office was seen as mediocre by comparison with his great friend, Pitt the Younger. In addition, his later incarnation as a reactionary Home Secretary led commentators to view him negatively. He was the first (upper) middle-class prime minister.

Henry was born in May 1757 and attended Winchester College and Oxford. His father, Doctor Anthony Addington, became a renowned physician who specialised in mental illness. He famously treated both Pitt the Elder and King George III and was responsible for prescribing port wine for the former's son. Henry and Pitt the Younger became good childhood friends.

Henry first entered parliament as a Tory MP in 1784 and failed to make much of an impression. However, in 1789 Pitt offered him the position of Speaker in the belief that he would be docile and supportive. In the event, this surprise appointment turned out well as Addington became highly respected and held the post for nearly twelve years. He was seen as fair-minded and he 'restored the dignity of the office'.

In 1801 Pitt resigned over the issue of Catholic emancipation. Both the king and Pitt had previously mooted the idea of Addington as a likely successor. Henry was at first reluctant to take over responsibilities as he was in such awe of his friend but eventually agreed. Once in office, however, he proved more adept than expected, although he was poor in debate and lacked any oratorical skills. He achieved a peace settlement (the Treaty of Amiens 1802) with Napoleonic France and won the ensuing election. Although the peace was extremely popular it was not to last. In May 1803 he invited some ridicule when he strode into the House dressed in the uniform of his local Berkshire militia to announce the resumption of hostilities with Napoleon. By now Pitt and his supporters felt that he should pass the mantle back to his friend to prosecute the war.

Amazingly, Addington agreed and over the next few months made various offers to step down but on certain conditions, none of which Pitt found acceptable. So he stayed on and introduced an excellent budget while conducting the war with reasonable aplomb. Eventually, however, in April 1804 parliamentary pressure forced Addington out and, reduced to a 'haggard neurotic', he resigned. He had been Prime Minister for three years and 54 days.

Afterwards, he moved to the House of Lords and became Viscount Sidmouth. He continued to serve in government and for ten years he was a rather unpopular Home Secretary who brought in repressive legislation and was later blamed for the infamous 'Peterloo Massacre' of 1819. He left office in 1824 but continued to oppose all reforms including Catholic emancipation in 1829 and the Great Reform Act of 1832. He died in February 1844 aged 86.

He was a man of great integrity and had been an able, if uninspiring, premier whose legacy has been tarnished by his reputation as an arch reactionary.

21. WILLIAM GRENVILLE WAS SATIRISED AS 'BOGEY'

William Grenville had the rare distinction of being able to follow his father, George Grenville, into the highest office. Only Pitt the Younger shared that honour. Incidentally, they were also first cousins. Like Addington, Grenville was a keen disciple of Pitt but was more independently minded. Overall, he was a very hard-working and able minister but, as he himself admitted, not really suited to the top job.

Unfortunately, later on in life he was viciously satirised by pamphleteers and cartoonists such as James Gillray. This was due to his appearance, which was rather goblin-like; he was described as having bulbous eyes and head, and a rather oversize posterior to match. He was cruelly dubbed Bogy, or Bogey.

Grenville was born in October 1759 and was descended from an ancient Norman family. Alas, he lost both his parents when aged 11 but he attended Eton and went on to Oxford where he excelled, receiving the Chancellor's Prize for best Latin Verse. He ventured into Parliament as a Whig in February 1782 at the age of 22 and joined the Grenvillite clan. His first appointment was as Chief Secretary to his brother, who was Lord Lieutenant of Ireland. William soon showed his abilities by personally piloting through Parliament the 'Renunciation Bill', which gave equality to the Irish parliament.

Pitt was impressed with this 'coming man' and they worked closely together. He appointed him Speaker in 1789 to help him out during the Regency crisis with George III and at just 29 he was the youngest person to hold the office since medieval times. Six months later he was appointed Home Secretary and was responsible for drawing up the Canada Act (1797) which divided the country into two provinces. Two years later he was switched to the House of Lords (as Lord Grenville) and took on the job of Foreign Secretary as well as Leader of the House.

He was now seen as Pitt's No 2 or 'vice chancellor' and helped direct the war against Napoleon from 1793 onwards.

In 1794 he negotiated the Jay Treaty over the American-Canadian border, which was the first use of arbitration. He followed Pitt out of office in 1801 but surprisingly ditched his old friend and refused to serve under Addington or Pitt later on. Upon Pitt's untimely demise in 1806 the king appointed him premier. Grenville had hoped to form a 'ministry of all the talents' but in the end he fielded a rather lacklustre team. As premier his efforts against Napoleon were generally defensive and instead his greatest success came with the abolition of the slave trade in March 1807. He lacked the necessary tact and charm and fell out with the king over the latter's staunch refusal to countenance Catholic emancipation. His government fell in the same month and had lasted one year and 42 days.

He mused afterwards, 'I am not competent in the management of men.' He lived to see Catholic emancipation finally enacted in 1829. He died five years later aged 74.

22. SPENCER PERCIVAL HELPED TO STOP THE SLAVE TRADE

Spencer Percival is famous for being the only prime minister to be assassinated. He has remained rather an unknown figure and was cruelly cut down in his prime. He was, in fact, a very worthy premier characterised by a strong evangelical Christianity.

He was born in November 1762. He had an unlucky start in life as his father died when he was only eight and his poor mother was left with 16 children to care for (from two marriages). He attended Harrow and Cambridge University, where he worked hard and eschewed drinking owing to his fervent religious views. His appearance was unusual as he was quite short with a sallow complexion. Indeed, he looked rather 'sepulchral', given his habit of wearing black.

In 1786 Percival qualified as a barrister and built up a steady business and he later served with the government's junior counsel for the prosecution of the radical Thomas Paine and his subversive book *The Rights of Man*. Afterwards, he became King's Counsel and upon entering Parliament he continued his legal work making the considerable sum of £10,000 a year by 1804.

In 1796 Percival was elected as MP for Northampton and immediately impressed Pitt with his brilliant speech making. He soon became one of the best government debaters, but it was not until Addington's premiership in 1801 that he was offered the post of Solicitor-General and later Attorney-General. His real breakthrough came in in 1807 when he was made Chancellor of the Exchequer and Leader of the Commons. For the next five years he encouraged a more expansionist stance against Napoleon and was responsible for supporting the Duke of Wellington in his long Peninsular War in Spain and Portugal, as well as providing the usual subsidies to European powers. Amazingly, despite the increased expenditure he managed to avoid tax increases through careful husbanding and long-term loans.

Portland's government fell in October 1809 and Percival was then asked to form the next administration. Unfortunately, few MPs were willing to serve under him and it took him six weeks to fill the nine-man cabinet. His government managed to survive various threats such as the disastrous Walcheren expedition in the Netherlands and the Regency crisis. In 1810, George III finally became irredeemably insane and there was apprehension that the Prince of Wales on becoming Regent would immediately call for the opposition Whigs to form a government. In the end, however, he fell out with them and preferred to retain Percival. By May 1812 he finally led a strong and stable government when he was suddenly struck down... (See below.)

Percival was 49 years old and had been Prime Minister for just two years and 221 days. Despite his achievements he had been a mostly conservative figure who had stood against parliamentary reform and Catholic emancipation. However, it should be noted that he had seen it as his moral duty to continue to stamp out the slave trade and had stepped up the Royal Navy presence off West Africa, thereby saving many thousands of lives.

23. HIS ASSASSIN WAS NOT A LUNATIC

The dramatic event took place in the lobby of the House of Commons on 11 May 1812. The murderer was John Bellingham, who had worked in Russia as an export representative but had got into debt through no fault of his own and had spent five years languishing in a prison there. He felt that the British ambassador to St Petersburg, Lord Granville Leveson-Gower, had done very little to support him and was demanding compensation from the British government. His requests went unheeded, however, and such was his resentment that he decided to direct his vengeance against the Prime Minister himself. He strode into the lobby and pointed his gun directly at Percival's chest and fired. 'I am murdered, murdered,' Percival cried.

Afterwards, Bellingham sat down calmly and awaited his arrest. There was cheering in the streets when news got out and crowds had to be beaten off when he was transported to Newgate prison. Three days later he was tried at the Old Bailey and a defence plea of insanity was lodged on his behalf. The accused addressed the court for two hours lucidly justifying his actions. It will come as no surprise then that the jury took a mere ten minutes to duly convict him of murder and he was hanged soon after.

Percival may not have been popular but the day after the shocking incident the House of Commons voted an annuity of £2000 for his widow and a grant of £50,000 for his 13 children. As for his assassin, his clothes were auctioned off and one punter offered £10 for his greatcoat.

24. THE EARL OF LIVERPOOL WAS A STEADY HAND AT THE TILLER

Robert Jenkinson, the 2nd Earl of Liverpool, was characterised by Benjamin Disraeli (future premier) as an arch-mediocrity, but this is undoubtedly an unfair assessment. Although he ranks as the third longest serving prime minister after Walpole and Pitt the Younger, he certainly does not qualify as one of the all-time greats. However, he was an excellent manager and conciliator and kept together a strong team when in office.

He was born in June 1770 but had a tragic start in life as his mother died a month later. He was educated at Charterhouse and then Oxford. During his Grand Tour he witnessed the opening events of the French Revolution (1789) including the fall of the Bastille. Thereafter he had an abiding 'distaste' for the mob.

Soon after entering Parliament in 1791, he made a perceptive and wide-ranging foreign policy speech which impressed Pitt. However, it was not until Addington in 1801 that he was offered the prestigious position of Foreign Secretary. At first, he was overawed by the role but soon showed himself to be a capable minister by negotiating the Treaty of Amiens with the French, which brought peace for 18 months. With Pitt's return in 1804 he was switched to the job of Home Secretary and Leader in the Lords having been ennobled as Baron Hawkesbury. Later under Spencer Percival he was made Secretary of State for War and the Colonies where he worked assiduously to support Wellington in Spain and Portugal. In 1809 his father died and he became the Earl of Liverpool.

In June 1812 he was the natural successor to Percival as Prime Minister. He was suitably Tory and highly experienced having held the great offices of state for many years. His immediate task was the war against Napoleon, which appeared to be successfully concluded in 1814. However, the French Emperor escaped from Elba a year later and the war continued. Liverpool intervened decisively to help the Duke of Wellington enlarge his standing army in the Netherlands from 4000 to 32,000, which came in handy at Waterloo.

Celebrations were short-lived as post-war problems soon piled up. Industrial and agricultural downturns led to high unemployment and the rise of radical demands for parliamentary reform. The threat of revolution appeared very real and *habeas corpus* was suspended in 1817. Two years later his government was vilified by many for the 'Peterloo Massacre' when local yeomanry were sent in and slaughtered 11 protesters at a mass open-air meeting. The 'Six Acts' followed, which curtailed the press and further protest meetings. However, the Cato Street Conspiracy (1820), a foiled plot to blow up the cabinet, showed that serious threats did exist.

After 1822 the economic situation improved and the era of 'Liberal Tory' government began. Reductions in tariffs allowed for greater free trade and permission for the formation of trade unions was granted. In February 1827 Liverpool suffered a massive cerebral haemorrhage and he was forced to resign. His administration had lasted for 14 years and 305 days. He died in December 1828 aged 58.

25. GEORGE CANNING WAS HIS OWN WORST ENEMY

The unlucky George Canning was the shortest-serving premier but also one of the ablest men to hold that esteemed position. However, his career is coloured by his tendency to cause offence to those around him and by his naked ambition. His lowly background meant it was remarkable that he was able to reach such an exalted position at all.

He was born in April 1770 to a minor Irish gentry family. His early years were tough as his father died on his first birthday and his young mother turned to acting to make ends meet. Remarkably, such a background did not inhibit his advancement in later life. At the age of eight, a wealthy uncle became his guardian and he was sent to Eton where he distinguished himself, co-editing a satirical magazine called *The Microcosm*. Canning made his own witty contributions, and such was the magazine's renown that it was read by George III and his wife, Queen Charlotte. He then went on to Oxford where he won the Chancellor's Medal for Latin verse.

After his studies he dallied with the idea of following a career in law, but he much preferred politics. With little means he brazenly wrote (aged 22) to the Prime Minister, Pitt the Younger, and invited himself for an interview. Pitt, knowing of his renown, agreed. The pair soon struck up a friendship with the result that Pitt found a seat for him in Parliament, as well as a junior post in the Foreign Office.

Despite his obvious abilities Canning managed to undermine his own cause by ill-judged comments and actions. He developed a close relationship with Princess Caroline, the estranged wife of the future George IV who suspected he was her lover and who henceforth was hostile to his advancement. After Pitt's resignation in 1801 Canning joined him on the backbenches but cruelly ridiculed his successor, Henry Addington, with the result that in later administrations the two were incapable of working together. At long last in 1807 he was offered the position of Foreign Secretary and organised the seizure of the Danish fleet under the nose of Napoleon. Regrettably, he argued with Lord Castlereagh of the War Office over the direction of the war and unsuccessfully demanded his removal. Two years later, in 1809, Castlereagh found out about his intriguing and challenged Canning to a duel on Putney Heath. He was left slightly injured but these events meant he remained outside government.

By 1822 a suitably chastened and less arrogant Canning was allowed back into the Foreign Office. He charmed the king and proved his worth a year later. When French troops invaded Spain, he immediately deployed the fleet to assist the Spanish colonies in South America, making him a popular hero there to this day.

After the resignation of Lord Liverpool in April 1827 Canning was at last given his chance in the top job. Alas, ill health overtook him, and he died after 119 days as premier. He was 57.

26. VISCOUNT GODERICH WAS KNOWN AS 'THE BLUBBERER'

Like his predecessor, George Canning, Viscount Goderich had a rather short-lived innings as premier. He held the top job for only four months. He was a well-liked, genial character who, however, was sometimes overcome by his emotions. Despite this weakness he managed a very long ministerial career, which stretched from 1809 to 1846.

He was born Frederick Robinson in October 1782 and came from a well-connected family. He passed through Harrow and Cambridge where he won a prize for the best Latin ode.

His first entry into Parliament came in 1806 and although nominally a Pittite he held independent views. Lord Castlereagh took him under his wing, and he was soon awarded a junior position as Under-Secretary in the Department of War and Colonies. In 1812 Castlereagh was made Foreign Secretary and the two became very involved in the Vienna settlement after the defeat of Napoleon. Upon his return Robinson was feted as a hero.

Soon after this he married a very wealthy heiress named Lady Sarah Hobart. From the financial viewpoint this worked out well, but with the passing of the years she became increasingly neurotic and unbalanced, and this had an unfortunate impact upon his career.

In 1815 England was still a mainly agricultural country and the aristocratic elite in Parliament demanded artificial protection for wheat prices through the controversial Corn Laws, thereby raising the cost of bread. Robinson had the unenviable task of introducing the Bill in the House of Commons. The reaction to this was immediate and the London mob was soon besieging his house. Soldiers were brought in and his butler took a pot shot at the crowd, killing a widow. Robinson was so distraught that he was reduced to tears when recounting the incident to Parliament.

All sides of the House of Commons saw him as amiable and hard-working and in 1822 he was rewarded with the post of

Chancellor of the Exchequer. By this time the economy was picking up after the downturn following the Napoleonic Wars. In fact, the country was booming and Robinson was able to offer tax cuts and sweeping tariff reductions in his budgets. He was soon dubbed 'Prosperity Robinson'. In 1827 Lord Liverpool left office. George Canning took over and made Robinson Leader in the Lords and ennobled him as Viscount Goderich. Shortly afterwards, however, Canning passed away.

George IV asked Goderich to take over in August. He found it frustratingly difficult to form a cabinet that would satisfy the Whigs and the king. Indeed, he went home every night and wept. He sent a note to the king informing him of the bickering and recriminations as well as his own acute domestic troubles making his 'health enfeebled'. George IV described Goderich as 'a damned, snivelling, blubbering blockhead'. The king immediately dissolved his government, much to the dismay of Goderich and during the painful interview that followed the king offered his handkerchief to mop up the inevitable 'waterworks'.

Although he was not suited to the highest office, he continued *in office* for many more years. He died in 1859 aged 76.

27. THE DUKE OF WELLINGTON WAS NOT A GREAT PRIME MINISTER

The Duke of Wellington was a rare instance in British history of a war hero taking the top political job. However, he found the position irksome as he was used to dishing out the orders and not having them questioned or discussed.

He was born Arthur Wesley (later Wellesley) in May 1769, which was the same year as his famous battlefield opponent Napoleon. After attending Eton, he joined the army aged 17 and devoted himself to playing cards, getting into debt, visiting brothels and playing the violin. After a few years, however, he decided to take soldiering seriously. In 1795 he was posted to India where he won a string of victories and for which he was knighted.

In 1805 he returned to marry his former sweetheart, Kitty. She had rejected him 12 years earlier on the grounds that he lacked sufficient income; he felt honour-bound to propose once more. This time she accepted, but in the meantime, she had aged somewhat and on the wedding day he remarked 'She has become ugly, by Jove!' It was not a good start.

Famously, Wellesley further enhanced his military reputation by beating Napoleon's armies in Spain for which he was made the Duke of Wellington. In June 1815 he won a 'damned near-run thing' at Waterloo. The Iron Duke was toasted across Europe as the greatest military commander of all time, 'the conqueror of conquerors'. He returned to Britain three years later and entered the House of Lords where he turned into a pin-up boy for the reactionary Tory ultras who baulked at any reform.

After the dismissal of Viscount Goderich King George IV asked the Duke to form an administration in January 1828. Ironically, as premier he then proceeded to bring in legislation which infuriated his erstwhile supporters. He repealed the Test and Corporations Act, which had excluded non-Anglican Protestants from public office and then he accepted that Catholic emancipation was necessary to avoid severe discontent in Ireland. One furious Tory, the Earl of Wichilsea, grossly libelled the Duke and a duel was fought on Battersea Fields in March 1829; both parties fired wide.

The death of George IV in June 1830 and the accession of William IV occasioned a general election that saw gains for the opposition Whigs. Wellington then showed himself out of touch by openly declaring himself against any reform when many were clamouring for it. Soon after, he lost a vote and resigned. His total time in office (including three weeks in 1834) was two years and 320 days.

The new Whig premier, Lord Grey, then introduced the long-awaited parliamentary reform bill which Wellington vehemently opposed. However, when in 1832 revolution seemed to be in the offing, he persuaded enough Tory lords to abstain thereby allowing it to become law. He had done the noble thing and backed down when duty required.

He had not been a great premier but nevertheless important reforms were passed on his watch. He died in 1852 aged 83.

28. EARL GREY WASN'T EVERYONE'S CUP OF TEA

It is true that a brand of tea was named after one of Britain's most important prime ministers. Supposedly, it was offered to the great man by a Chinese mandarin. However, he should also be remembered as the premier who was responsible for the Great Reform Act, which ushered politics into the modern era, as well as the abolition of slavery throughout the British Empire.

Charles Grey was born in March 1764 into an ancient aristocratic family based in Northumberland and dating back to the fourteenth century. He was educated at Eton and Cambridge and afterwards did the usual Grand Tour. In 1786 a seat in Parliament was found for him by an uncle and Grey was expected to support the Tory government led by Pitt the Younger. Instead, he veered towards the moderate reforming Whigs led by Charles James Fox, who espoused parliamentary reform and Catholic emancipation.

Politics aside, Grey greatly enjoyed the company of Whig hostesses, in particular the renowned beauty of the day, Giorgiana, Duchess of Devonshire. They got on so well that she bore him a daughter. Later on, he married Mary Elizabeth Ponsonby who gave birth to 16 children. This total stands as a record for any prime minister ... so far.

The Tories dominated government in this period but an opportunity for the opposition Whigs occurred when Grenville (21) formed his 'Ministry of all the Talents' in 1806-7. Grey was offered the post of First Lord of the Admiralty and later Foreign Secretary and Leader of the Commons. During this time, he was responsible for piloting through the legislation abolishing the slave trade.

In 1806 Fox died and Grey assumed the leadership of the Whigs for the next 27 years – most of it in opposition! One major reason for this was King George IV's acute dislike of him.

By 1830 Grey was aged 66 and risked becoming just a footnote in history. However, the mood of the country had suddenly changed and there was now an overwhelming demand for parliamentary reform. George IV died that year and the new King, William IV, soon asked Grey to form an administration.

He quickly brought in a reform bill which narrowly passed through the Commons but was blocked by the Tory-dominated House of Lords. Grey called an election which gave him a sizeable majority in the Commons but again the Bill was blocked in the Lords. There was a real possibility of revolution and the king threatened to 'pack' the House of Lords with 60 Whig peers if the Bill was blocked again. This forced the Tories to let the Bill pass in April 1832. A year later his government abolished slavery in the British Empire and a Factory Act brought about better conditions. An Act bringing in workhouses was also passed.

Grey retired in July 1834. His administration had lasted three years and 229 days. He died aged 81 in 1845. Despite Grey's mighty achievements he remained throughout an aristocrat who believed in only limited 'necessary reform'.

29. THE GREAT REFORM ACT CHANGED EVERYTHING

Earl Grey's Great Reform Act was greater and more far reaching than he could have realised. He saw it as modernising and improving an outdated and corrupt system in order to avoid revolution. He expected the act to be a one-off reform, but his Tory opponents rightly saw it as the thin edge of the wedge, as it set a precedent for future reform bills which would result in all classes (including the wretched working classes!) being enfranchised.

What did the act achieve? Firstly, as many as 140 'rotten boroughs' seats (see fact 1) were abolished. These boroughs, mostly in southern England, had retained their right to return two MPs despite their populations having moved away over the previous centuries. For example, Old Sarum and Gatton each had an electorate of seven while Dunwich had disappeared into the sea! The act now mostly redistributed these seats to new cities in the industrialised north. In addition, the growing middle class was given the vote thereby expanding the electorate from 11 to 18 per cent of the adult male population.

An important result of all this was that elections were now properly contested events with the choice of the majority party and prime minister decisively in the hands of the people. Monarchs could not now select a premier of their personal choice but had to follow the will of the electorate. It marked a seismic change. A final point is that the parties were forced to modernise in order to appeal to a new national electorate. Tories soon preferred to call themselves Conservatives and some Whigs called themselves Liberals.

30. VISCOUNT MELBOURNE WAS A SURROGATE FATHER FOR THE QUEEN

William Lamb, 2nd Viscount Melbourne, was a gifted and intelligent man but was plagued by indecisiveness and an intense dislike of confrontation. He is remembered for a disastrous marriage and his close relationship with the young Queen Victoria.

William was born in March 1779. He was the second child of a vivacious and rather promiscuous mother. Altogether the parents had six children but only the first-born was truly the father's and the rest were from different lovers of the mother. One of William's brothers, George, was probably the offspring of the future George IV and William himself was allegedly fathered by the Earl of Egremont. The first Viscount didn't question the parentage and they were all brought up together in the family home.

William went to Eton, Cambridge and Glasgow University and afterwards was called to the Bar. He first entered Parliament at the age of 26 but made little impression there. His elder brother suddenly died in 1801 which made William heir to the estate. As a result of this, he was able to marry Lady Caroline Ponsonby with whom he was deeply in love. Unfortunately, she proved wayward and impetuous and indulged in a string of open affairs culminating in a scandalous liaison with the notorious Lord Byron, which included a mock wedding ceremony. Eventually, Melbourne was obliged to separate from her, but he remained close to her until her death in 1828.

The year 1827 saw his fortunes take a turn. Having drifted in life somewhat, he was suddenly offered the position of First Secretary of Ireland by Prime Minister George Canning. At 48 he revelled in his first real job, and he found he had a capacity for hard work. His success there led to another surprise appointment as Home Secretary under Earl Grey in 1830.

Although nominally a Whig, Melbourne was deeply conservative in outlook despite being part of Grey's reforming ministry. He was certainly not a great enthusiast for parliamentary reform and heartily disliked the middle classes who had recently acquired the vote. William IV shared this conservatism and so he appointed him Prime Minister in July 1834. After four months the king dismissed him, but he returned in May 1835.

Melbourne's governments lasted for six years and 255 days but achieved little of substance. The hated Poor Law Amendment Act (passed by Grey's government) was implemented leading to bitter opposition to the new workhouses. In June 1837 the 18-year-old Queen Victoria came to the throne and Melbourne took on the role of father-counsellor. She was delighted to have him as a guiding hand and called him her 'good friend'. He became a de facto private secretary and by some accounts would spend as much as six hours at court a day. This cosy relationship slowly came to an end after she married Prince Albert in 1840.The following year Melbourne lost the election and resigned.

His last few years were dogged by ill health and he finished a sad and lonely figure. He died in November 1848 aged 69.

31. SIR ROBERT PEEL CAUSED A DRAMATIC SPLIT IN THE TORY PARTY

Sir Robert Peel is unique within the prime ministerial annals as he came from a northern manufacturing background. Indeed, throughout his life he spoke with a Lancashire accent, and he undoubtedly felt socially isolated amongst the lords and ladies of the day.

He was born in February 1788 and was the eldest of 11 children. Both his grandfather and father were self-made men in the Lancashire cotton industry, and his father was keen for him to be a gentleman so packed him off to Harrow and Oxford, where he was the first student to achieve a Double First in Humanities and Mathematics.

The young Robert was soon found a seat in Parliament (1809) and immediately impressed with his maiden speech. Within a year he was offered a position in government as an under-secretary before being made Chief Secretary for Ireland in 1812. After 10 years he was raised to the position of Home Secretary. Fearful of revolution he is forever remembered for creating the Metropolitan Police Force for London, with the result that policemen were afterwards known as 'Peelers' or 'Bobbies'. He designed the dark blue serge uniform to be unthreatening and decidedly non-military. Each officer sported a top hat and a truncheon.

After the fall of Wellington in 1830 Peel was made Tory Party leader, a post he held for the next 20 years. He accepted Whig reforms and set about modernising the party. In the 1834 election he issued the Tamworth Manifesto, which declared the new Conservative Party as being one of 'caution and common sense'.

After a short stint as Prime Minister from December 1834 to April 1835 he was returned to power in 1841. It was to be one of the most important premierships in history. To begin with, things went well. The massive national debt was turned into a surplus through income tax, with some of the revenue going towards tariff reductions, thus taking Britain further on the road to free trade. However, the failure of the Irish potato crop in 1845 created a calamitous situation with the loss of at least a million lives there. Peel needed to import cheap grain to alleviate the crisis but was thwarted by the Corn Laws (the 'Bread Tax') which kept grain prices artificially high, and which suited Tory landowners. Peel decided they were no longer defensible and pushed a Bill through Parliament abolishing them. A massive Tory revolt followed with 231 of his own party voting against it, and it was only with the support of the Whigs that the Bill passed. The Conservatives were now fatally split, with Peelites sitting separately in the Commons. Peel resigned and the Conservatives were to remain out of power for a generation. He had been Prime Minister for five years and 57 days. In July 1850 he died after a riding accident. He was 62.

For some, Peel was a hero who put country before party but for others he was a traitor. The repercussions for British politics were tectonic.

32. LORD JOHN RUSSELL WAS BOTH A WHIG AND A LIBERAL

Lord John Russell was a strong driving force for reform in many areas of public life. His achievements were impressive, but he probably could have achieved more but for his haughtiness and cavalier disregard for his colleagues.

He was born in August 1792 to a strongly Whiggish aristocratic family. He was a sickly child who grew up to be short in stature (five feet four inches) and although ill health plagued him throughout his life he lived to a ripe old age. He was mostly schooled at home due to his frailty but did attend Westminster School for a short while and went on to Edinburgh University. He travelled extensively in Spain and Portugal during the Napoleonic Wars and in 1814 visited Elba, where he had an interview with Napoleon.

He was elected to Parliament at the age of 21 but for many years his focus was writing. His many works included various histories, a novel and a play in verse. However, by the 1820s zeal for parliamentary reform overtook him and he became a leading orator for the cause. His reward was a position as Postmaster General for the Armed Forces in Grey's 1830 government. However, his real job was on the committee tasked with drawing up what would become the Great Reform Act of 1832. He became the main proponent for the government and steadfastly helped to push the Bill through against bitter opposition. It was perhaps Lord John's 'finest hour'.

He stayed on in Melbourne's administration when as Home Secretary (and Leader of the Commons) he helped Catholics into public offices in Ireland and reduced the number of crimes which incurred the death penalty. By 1841 the Whigs were out of office and Russell was Melbourne's clear successor as party leader.

In June 1846 he became Prime Minister of a minority Whig government kept in office by a combination of Conservative Peelites (see previous fact), radicals and Irish MPs. A raft of small reforms was brought in covering public health, the

10-hour working day for women and children, and education. However, the key issue facing the government was the continuing Irish potato famine, which his government failed to adequately confront. His aloofness and inability to consult or develop close relationships undermined his support and his government fell in February 1852.

After a short-lived Conservative administration, he expected to return as premier but his colleagues much preferred to support the Earl of Aberdeen, a Peelite. He continued to serve in successive administrations but was largely side-lined. Despite this, he was instrumental in the creation of the new Liberal Party in June 1859.

After the death of Palmerston in July 1865 Russell formed his second administration aged 73. His desire for reform was undiminished but his Second Reform Bill which partly enfranchised the working classes was defeated by 11 votes in June 1866. (Eventually a more radical version was passed by the Tories the following year.) He subsequently resigned for the last time. In total he was premier for six years and 111 days. He died aged 86 in May 1878.

33. THE 14TH EARL OF DERBY BELIEVED IN 'MASTERLY INACTIVITY'

The Earl of Derby's career was indeed remarkable, not for its achievements but rather for its relative failure after so much early promise. He was leader of the Conservative party for 22 years, a record, and was the first prime minister to form three administrations. Unfortunately, all three were short-lived minority governments.

He was born in March 1799 as Edward Stanley to a pedigree aristocratic family which traced its origins back to 1485 and Bosworth Field. He was an excellent scholar at both Eton and Oxford and was elected to Parliament as a Whig aged just 23. He was soon recognised for his excellent speech-making and was eagerly welcomed into Grey's administration in 1830 where, as Secretary for War and the Colonies, he was instrumental in pushing through the Abolition of Slavery Bill. By now he was so esteemed that he was tipped as the next Whig prime minister but rashly resigned over an issue concerning Ireland and the opportunity passed.

In any case, by 1835 he felt closer to Sir Robert Peel and the Tories than the Whigs and three years afterwards formally defected to them. In 1841 Peel gave him his old job back as Colonial Secretary and, in this guise, he had the honour of formally annexing Hong Kong from the Chinese. However, the cosy relationship with Peel did not last as he disagreed with his scrapping of the Corn Laws in 1846, which was to end up causing that fatal split in the party. The remaining Tories who did not follow Peel soon rallied round Lord Stanley (as he now was) and he became leader with the major remit of reuniting the party. In this he was not wholly successful, but he was able to slowly rebuild the party with the help of his able lieutenant Benjamin Disraeli, who represented the party in the Commons.

Although Stanley was to retain control of the party for the next two decades there were mutterings and criticism of his laid-back leadership style, which he described as 'masterly inactivity'. Hunting and shooting seemed more appealing than winning power. His first term as premier came unexpectedly in February 1852 but as Derby (as he now was after the death of his father) lacked a majority he promptly called an election, which the Tories lost, so he just as promptly resigned. Another opportunity to form an administration followed in February 1858, again without a majority; its main achievement was to create the British Raj by bringing India under direct government control. Another election was called and this time the Tories did rather better but not enough to stay in government, so he resigned once more in June 1859.

The last chance came in June 1866 as always in a minority. This time, together with Disraeli, he boldly pushed through the Second Reform Act, which included working class voters for the first time. In February 1868, struggling with gout and ill-health, he resigned. In total he had been in government for three years and 280 days. He died in October 1869.

34. THE EARL OF ABERDEEN WAS NOT A WAR LEADER

George Gordon, 4th Earl of Aberdeen, had an unusual parliamentary career as he never set foot in the House of Commons. This turned out to be a handicap as he was not baptised into the cut and thrust of debate that is a feature of the place, and this no doubt contributed to his being a poor speaker. If all could agree that he was a good man, he was certainly not a good war leader, which was unfortunate at the time of the Crimean war (1853-6).

He was born in January 1784 to an ancient aristocratic Scottish family. His life was to be often touched by tragedy and early on he lost both his parents. He was lucky, however, as Henry Dundas, a family friend, and Pitt the Younger financed his education at Harrow and Cambridge. He followed this up with an extensive Grand Tour during an intermission in the Napoleonic Wars in 1802. This included a trip to France where he was given the honour of dining with Napoleon. Afterwards he went on to Constantinople and Greece where he became very involved in archaeological digs, afterwards becoming an expert on antiquities. He participated with Lord Elgin in removing some reliefs from the Acropolis.

He married in 1805 but his young wife died in 1810 and his son and three daughters all died before the age of 20, which he deeply lamented for the rest of his life. His second marriage was also unhappy as they lived mainly separate lives until she, too, died in 1833, although some children did survive this time. No wonder his hair fell out!

In 1813 he personally witnessed and was horrified by the Battle of Leipzig in which 100,000 soldiers died and this left him something of a pacifist. After 1815 he mainly devoted himself to his family and his academic pursuits and it was not until 1841 that he became Foreign Secretary in Sir Robert Peel's administration. Aberdeen stayed loyal to Peel and became leader of the Peelite faction after the leader's demise in 1850 and two years later he himself became premier. It was felt his personality would help bring together the unwieldy coalition of Whigs, Peelites and Irish MPs. The ministry soon became embroiled in a protracted war in the Crimea. France and Britain sent a sizeable army to the Black Sea peninsula with the intention of pushing back Russia and safeguarding the Turkish Empire. The British army was clearly not fit for purpose with huge losses and inefficiencies coming to light. Aberdeen spoke poorly in defence of his handling of the war and lost a key vote, resulting in his resignation in January 1855.

Perhaps it came as a relief. 'I consider war to be the greatest folly,' he once declared. His premiership had lasted two years and 42 days. He died aged 76 in 1860. He was ill-suited to politics in general and was scapegoated for the failures of others.

35. THE LIBERAL PARTY WAS A BROAD CHURCH

The Liberal Party was officially formed in the Willis's Tea Rooms in St James's Street, London, on 6 June 1859. It brought together the disparate factions that had previously combined on an ad hoc basis to create anti-Tory governments, but which made the politics of the day rather unstable. Whigs, Peelites and Radicals agreed to combine into one party, but they were not necessarily happy bedfellows. The Radicals wanted to see much more extensive social and parliamentary reforms than their more conservative, aristocratic, partners. However, they did all agree on the importance of free trade and equal rights for those of different Christian beliefs.

It was decided that the first Liberal prime minister should be the ageing but charismatic Lord Palmerston. He was an ex-Tory who skilfully avoided any major reforms that included extension of the vote. Some see Gladstone as the first real Liberal premier as he brought in a whole raft of measures, which included education for all as well as various parliamentary reforms. In 1905 the Liberals won a landslide election and under Asquith (and Lloyd George as Chancellor of the Exchequer) pensions were introduced, which heralded the beginnings of the welfare state. This was to be the heyday of the party as after 1918 the Liberals fell into decline due to the rise of the Labour Party and bitter internal divisions. Thereafter they were fated to be a third party squeezed between Conservatives and Labour.

In March 1988 the Liberals merged with the Social Democrats to form the Liberal Democrats (Lib Dems).

36. LORD PALMERSTON WAS THE FIRST POPULIST POLITICIAN

Lord Palmerston was one of the most colourful and popular politicians of the nineteenth century. Outside Parliament he was often seen as a great hero but was much more distrusted inside. His support amongst the public was also undoubtedly enhanced by his reputation with the fair sex. Palmerston's record of 48 years of ministerial posts in government remains unequalled and throughout this time he displayed enormous stamina and impressive command of his briefs (no connection intended with the previous sentence!). At the age of 70 he was also the oldest person to be premier for the first time.

Henry John Temple was born in October 1784 into an Irish peerage with estates in both Ireland and England. He attended Harrow, Edinburgh and Cambridge where he shone academically. Upon entering Parliament, he immediately joined the Tory government in a junior post but within a couple of years he gained promotion as Secretary at War, basically a glorified auditor for the armed forces. He was soon noted as an excellent administrator but remained stuck in the job for the next 18 years! He could never give a satisfactory explanation for this, but cynics suggested it was because he enjoyed London society too much.

By the 1820s he felt that he had more in common with reforming Whigs than the Tories and in 1828 resigned from Wellington's hard-line government. As if released from all previous constraints he suddenly regaled Parliament with some expert orations on foreign policy. It was on the back of these that he was offered the position of Foreign Secretary in Grey's 1830 Whig government. He soon revealed himself as a master of diplomacy, shifting support between different countries and leaders to suit British interests, declaring that Britain had 'no eternal enemies or friends'.

Palmerston's first problem in office was to deal with the Belgian revolt against Holland. In 1830 he hosted the London Conference with all the Great Powers of Europe taking part and by a clever mix of promises and threats managed to get them to agree to a long-term settlement. It took a great deal of time, however, until everybody was on board, and it wasn't until 1839 that the final Treaty of London was signed and sealed. Not only was Belgian neutrality guaranteed by all the Great Powers, but a Belgian king was installed who suited both Britain and France. It was the breach of this neutrality which triggered Britain's entry into the First World War in 1914. Overall, it was nevertheless perhaps Palmerston's greatest achievement.

Another success in the 1830s was the Mehemet Ali affair. Ali was an Egyptian leader who threatened the Ottoman (Turkish) leadership in Constantinople. A client of France he had moved north and seized Syria. Palmerston forced him to withdraw by making an alliance with Russia, Austria and Prussia. France was furious and threatened war but in the end was obliged to beat a humiliating retreat as well. For some Whigs it was an exercise in reckless brinkmanship, which led to calls for his removal.

37. ... AND WAS AN EXPONENT OF GUNBOAT DIPLOMACY

One of the more controversial policies of Lord Palmerston was his habit of deploying the Royal Navy when he felt British citizens and British prestige had in some way been threatened or dishonoured.

An early example of this was the First Opium War with China in 1835. In the nineteenth century China was in a backward and weak state and was prey to the European powers. At this time the Chinese government was trying to stamp out the use of opium amongst its people. Much of it was being smuggled in by British merchants and when some of them were arrested and the opium was confiscated by the Chinese, it sparked a confrontation. Palmerston did not dispute that the actions of the merchants were illegal but considered the arrest and imprisonment of Englishmen an affront and demanded compensation and their release. The fleet was duly despatched, and Canton was bombarded, thereby forcing the Chinese to eventually agree to humiliating terms. By the Treaty of Nanking in 1842, China was obliged to pay $20 million and to cede the island of Hong Kong in compensation.

Another illustration of this policy came nearer to home. Don Pacifico was a Portuguese Jew who had been born in Gibraltar and who could therefore claim British citizenship. In 1850 he was living in Athens and had the misfortune to have his house burnt down in a riot there. He demanded a huge sum of money in compensation. Palmerston took up the case and sent in a naval squadron to blockade some Greek ports until the case was settled appropriately. There were heated protests from other European countries and in Parliament. It seemed that this time Palmerston had overstepped the mark and seemingly faced defeat in the House of Commons. However, he rose to the occasion by speaking for four hours and making one of his finest speeches. He defended his policy with the words '*Civis Romanus sum*' (I am a Roman citizen). Like the ancient Romans, he declared, British citizens wherever they may be should feel confident that the 'strong arm of England' would protect them. He won the vote, his popularity soared and the Greeks paid up (but not the full sum).

Not everybody approved of his policy. Some noted that he was a bully to the weak but a coward when confronted by the strong. Indeed, it is true that he would never have behaved in the same way with one of the Great Powers of Europe or the United States of America. Queen Victoria and Albert certainly thought his foreign policy too high-handed, and she had demanded to see all his despatches before they were sent.

Eventually, he fell foul of his royal critics. In December 1851 Louis-Napoleon overthrew the Second French Republic in a coup which a year later led to his enthronement as Napoleon III. Queen Victoria saw the Frenchman as an upstart adventurer and so when Palmerston immediately congratulated him, without government approval, she demanded Palmerston's removal from office. The Prime Minister agreed and sacked him.

38. PAM RESCUES BRITAIN IN THE CRIMEA

Palmerston was not out of office for long, as he was a powerful and influential figure. Queen Victoria had ruled him out of the Foreign Office, so he was offered the Home Office in Aberdeen's new government in 1852. He brought in some moderate reforms but adamantly refused to countenance further parliamentary reform that would extend the vote.

The Aberdeen government drifted into war against Russia in the Crimea in 1853. As mentioned before, Aberdeen failed to handle the war well and there was a popular clamour for Palmerston to take over the job. Much to Queen Victoria's irritation, she agreed to appoint him on 5 February 1855.

Even though he was 70 years of age he injected energy into the British war effort and improved the logistical and medical support for the troops. In particular, he gave his full backing to the work of Florence Nightingale. To his chagrin it was the French who secured final victory by taking the Malakoff Fortress and the new Russian Tsar, Alexander II, agreed to sign a Peace Treaty in Paris in March 1856. Palmerston was not able to impose the harsher terms he had hoped for but nevertheless painted it as a triumph and he was awarded an order of the Garter by the Queen.

In 1858 'Pam', as he was known by some of his adoring press, was unexpectedly ousted from office. For once he had lost his touch, as Parliament believed he was trying to appease the French Emperor after an assassination attempt and voted down a government Bill. However, he was soon back in office having now become the standard bearer of the recently formed Liberal Party. In June of that year, at the age of 76, he formed his last administration.

As might be expected, extensive reforms were off the table and the focus was on foreign policy. Although he retained remarkable mental clarity and stamina for a man of his age, his colleagues were aware he was slowing down. Sometimes in the House of Commons or in cabinet meetings he fell asleep, but he was not alone as some of his ministers also nodded off – it being the oldest cabinet in history!

His final years were not marked by diplomatic triumphs. Most humiliating was the failure of his 'gunboat diplomacy' in the Schleswig-Holstein affair. The two duchies belonged to Denmark but were rightly due to be inherited by a minor German king. Denmark disputed this but Austria and Prussia threatened war. Palmerston unwisely declared that Denmark would 'not fight alone' threatening to send in the fleet but the wily Prussian Chancellor, Otto von Bismarck, called his bluff. When Prussian and Austrian troops entered the duchies Palmerston lamely failed to act. Parliament was in uproar, but he somehow survived a vote of censure. Pam was reported to have said, 'Only three people have ever really understood the Schleswig-Holstein business – the Prince Consort, who is dead – a German professor, who has gone mad – and I, who have forgotten all about it.' This is surely one of the funniest quotes from any PM.

In October 1865 he caught a chill whilst out driving and died aged 80. He had been prime minister for nine years and 141 days. Abroad he was a heroic patriot but at home he had been a bulwark against reform.

39. PALMERSTON WAS AN INCORRIGIBLE LORD CUPID

Palmerston's amours certainly did no harm to his political career and may even have helped it. Such was his renown that he was dubbed 'Lord Cupid'. In his early years as a minister, he was invited to join an exclusive London club called Almack's. Of course, to gain entry you had to be a lady or gentleman, but the final decision rested with seven flirtatious lady patronesses. Our hero passed the test and three of them became his mistress. One of these, Lady Cowper, happened to be the sister of Lord Melbourne, so when Palmerston later married her, he became brother-in-law to the Prime Minister. Apparently, her first husband had been rather easy-going and unaware that three of his children were almost certainly sired by Palmerston.

Queen Victoria was definitely 'not amused' by an incident in 1839 while he was staying in Windsor Castle. She was shocked to hear that in the dead of night he had attempted to sneak into the room of a Lady-in-Waiting, who managed to raise the alarm, obliging his lordship to beat a hasty retreat.

In June 1863 there was an accusation that very much redounded to his favour. The husband of Mrs O'Kane cited Palmerston (then aged 79) as co-respondent in a divorce case and demanded damages of £20,000 for his dastardly behaviour with her. In the end the case was dismissed, as it turned out the O'Kanes were not even married. The case drew much amusement and interest throughout the country: 'The lady was certainly Kane, but was Palmerston Abel?'

40. DISRAELI STARTED OUT AS A DOUBLE-DEALING DANDY

Benjamin Disraeli has gone down in history as one of the two great titans of the nineteenth century (The other being Gladstone). Disraeli's rise to the top job is, on paper, rather improbable as he had huge obstacles to overcome. Firstly, there was strong anti-Semitic prejudice at the time; the second obstacle was his untrustworthiness and recklessness, which blighted his career for many years.

He was born in December 1804 to a wealthy family by the name of D'Israeli. His father, Isaac, decided to baptise his children into the Church of England, which proved fortunate for Benjamin's career. Disraeli's education was somewhat neglected as he left school at 15 and decided not to attend university. Instead, he dallied with the idea of working in a solicitor's office or training in law but in the end felt that fame, writing and politics were more his calling. By the age of 20 he had dropped the apostrophe in his surname and had taken to dressing up in a rather outlandish way, his hair in artificially created ringlets.

The publisher John Murray took an interest in Disraeli and his writing. Murray was lured by him into buying South American mining shares that subsequently crashed and then into putting capital into a newspaper of Disraeli's entitled *The Representative*. This, too, ended in complete failure (in 1825), leaving Disraeli deeply in debt and Murray having to sell his two houses in London. In an attempt to regain some of his losses, Disraeli wrote a book, *Vivien Grey*, which satirised Murray and others. Murray was naturally furious, and it is little wonder that Disraeli developed a reputation for double-dealing and insincerity.

As time went by his debts would rise to as much as £60,000 (£2½ million today). Until his election as an MP he was often fearful of his creditors and once he hid down a well to escape a sheriff's officer.

Politics were his consuming ambition, so he ingratiated himself into high society and, with the help of a Tory peer, eventually won a seat in Maidstone in 1837. His maiden speech soon after was a disaster, met with 'hoots, hisses, laughter and catcalls'. However, upon sitting down he declared that 'The time will come when you hear me.'

This was indeed the case as Disraeli's oratory and ability to enthral MPs for hours on end impressed the Tory leader, Sir Robert Peel. After the Conservatives won the 1841 election Disraeli expected to be included in the new government and was dismayed when he was left out. Five years later he had his revenge on Peel over his divisive repeal of the Corn Laws. Disraeli laid into him with such ferocity that it undoubtedly helped create a split so deep that the remaining Tories (and Disraeli) stayed effectively in opposition for the next 28 years. The event was a landmark in his career.

41. DIZZY REACHES THE TOP OF THE 'GREASY POLE'

Dizzy, as Disraeli was known by his friends and admirers, now became the leading figure for the Conservatives in the House of Commons, but he would have to wait many years to achieve actual leadership of the party. There were many amongst the Tories who disliked and distrusted him and yet, with his oratory and outstanding debating skills, he was indispensable to them. A typical example of opinions in the party is that of Lord Cecil who described him as 'an adventurer, a mere political gangster…without principles and honesty'. So, Lord Derby was appointed as overall leader while Disraeli became his able second in command, a situation that lasted for two decades.

Disraeli became shadow Leader of the House and Chancellor of the Exchequer. To match his new positions, he changed his image, disposing of his dandyish clothes and dressing sombrely in black; slowly, he was able to command more respect.

The Tories were in office with three short minority governments in 1855, 1858-9 and 1866-8 in which Disraeli was Chancellor and finally Prime Minister for the first time (in February 1868) when Derby retired. In 1867 Dizzy had skilfully steered through the radical Second Reform Bill, which gave some of the working class the vote for the first time. He hoped the Tories would be rewarded for this in the 1868 election but instead the Liberals were re-elected.

Disraeli would have to wait for a further six years before forming a majority government, by which time he was nearly 70. Plagued by ill-health he complained that power had come too late. From the start he made it clear that his focus would be on foreign and imperial affairs leaving hard-working members of his cabinet to bring in a slew of social reforms to compete with the Liberals under Gladstone. Of particular note were two Factory Acts and the Conspiracy and the Protection of Property Act, which legitimised peaceful picketing. For the first time the working classes could see the Tories as a viable alternative, and this was supported by a miners' leader who noted that the Conservatives had 'done more for the working class in five years than the Liberals in fifty'. That's a Dizzy height.

Dizzy's foreign policy was glitzy and patriotic. In 1875 he bought 40% shares in the Suez Canal from under the noses of the French. In the Congress of Berlin in 1878 he joined the Great Powers in forcing Russia to give up its recent gains in the Balkans and walked away with Cyprus claiming, 'Peace with Honour'. He made Queen Victoria Empress of India, much to her delight, and he was later ennobled as the Earl of Beaconsfield.

Alas, the end of his administration saw failed harvests and defeats in Zululand and Afghanistan resulting in his being ousted from office in the 1880 election. Suffering from gout, asthma and bronchitis, he died the following year aged 76. He was Prime Minister for six years and 339 days. Perhaps not a great premier, he did recast the image of the Tory party.

42. DISRAELI FLATTERED THE QUEEN

Disraeli once said that when it comes to royalty you have to lay on the flattery 'with a trowel' and he certainly did that. Queen Victoria undoubtedly enjoyed the romantic phraseology used by her Prime Minister addressing her sometimes as the 'Faerie Queen' or 'Queen Titania'. At the beginning of audiences he would kneel, kiss hands and say 'In loving loyalty and faith'.

To begin with she was suspicious of him and described him as 'not respectable' but his impressive eulogy to Prince Albert upon the death of the Prince Consort did much to win her over. After that he worked assiduously to win her respect, writing regular detailed and entertaining descriptions of the day's business in Parliament. She looked forward to his visits and compared him favourably with the 'straitlaced' and 'half-crazy' Liberal leader Gladstone. Dizzy had already written several novels but when the queen had her own work published entitled *Leaves from the journal of our life in the Highlands* in 1868, he delighted her by referring to 'We authors, ma'am'. The highest accolade came later with the creation of the queen as Empress of India and thereafter she was proud to sign off her correspondence with VRI (*Victoria Regina et Imperatrix*).

Victoria was distraught when Disraeli lost office in 1880 and was very concerned about his failing health. In his final weeks she wrote him numerous letters and sent flowers. She wanted to visit him in his Hughenden estate, but he decided against it saying, 'No, it is better not. She would only ask me to take a message to Albert.'

43. GLADSTONE WAS 'THE PEOPLE'S WILLIAM'

William Ewart Gladstone had an incredible career which stretched for over 62 years and included 27 years as a minister. He was a formidable Chancellor of the Exchequer as well as Prime Minister and his actions in government were generally guided by his deeply held religious beliefs and his desire for social justice. When he finally left office at the age of 84 he was to make history as the oldest prime minister upon retirement. He is also remembered for his nearly three-decade long rivalry with the Tory leader Benjamin Disraeli from 1852 to 1881. They were the two titans of the Victorian era.

William was born in December 1809 and was educated at Eton and Oxford. His family were devoutly religious and belonged to the evangelical wing of the Church of England and this greatly affected him throughout his life. At university he was noted for his debating prowess and was elected president of the Oxford Union.

Aged just 22 he was elected to parliament as a Tory MP. At this time, he was against all reform and in his maiden speech he even spoke against the abolition of slavery as his father was a slave-holder in Jamaica. He was seen as 'the rising hope of those stern and unbending Tories' and was soon offered a post in Peel's Conservative government in 1841. Two years later he held the cabinet post of President of the Board of Trade where he opened up travel by forcing the railway companies to offer cheaper fares. He subsequently left the Tories along with Peel.

His phenomenal stamina and powers of concentration were soon noted by those in cabinet. One member commented that 'Gladstone could do in four hours what it took any other man sixteen to do and he [nonetheless] worked sixteen hours a day'!

By 1852 his forensic destruction of Disraeli's budget meant that he was the natural choice for Chancellor of the Exchequer in Aberdeen's government soon after. His first budget speech in 1853 lasted nearly five hours and produced a modern, detailed account of the nation's finances for the first time. As in all his 11 budgets that followed, he was determined to reduce duties on imported goods and increase free trade. He also later attempted to abolish income tax but failed due to the Crimean War (1853-6) and his abolition of paper duties meant that the press was more affordable and could now be read more widely. The grateful *Daily Telegraph* dubbed him 'the People's William'.

By 1859 he was a fully paid-up member of the new Liberal Party and continued as Chancellor under Palmerston and Lord John Russell. In 1866 Gladstone was tasked with introducing a new reform bill that would extend the vote to some of the working classes. The Bill had little support in the Commons and was voted down. The Tories took over and passed a more radical act and expected to be rewarded by the people in the 1868 election. They weren't.

44. IRELAND BECAME HIS OBSESSION

The 1868 election was another victory for the Liberal party, and with the retirement of Lord John Russell, Gladstone was the overwhelming favourite to succeed as prime minister. It was to be the first of four administrations – a record so far. Upon being informed that he would be asked to form the next government he declared, 'My mission is to pacify Ireland.' The country was suffering constant outbreaks of violence resulting from the wretched living conditions imposed on the Irish people. He felt it was his moral duty to eradicate those grievances.

Gladstone's first government started life in December 1868 and lasted until February 1874. It was to be one of the finest reforming ministries of the nineteenth century but surprisingly little was achieved regarding Ireland. The landmark reforms included the 1870 Education Act, which secured education for all up to the age of 12, and the 1872 Ballot Act that allowed for secret voting in elections for the first time. Advancement by merit was encouraged in the army and the Home Office clearing the way for much greater efficiency in these areas.

After the loss of power in 1874 Gladstone apparently lapsed into semi-retirement and gave the impression that his career was finished. However, after the horror of the Turkish massacres in Bulgaria in 1876 he unleashed a barnstorming campaign against the Tories that eventually swept him back into office in 1880.

The second administration saw a more radical and reckless Gladstone. Apart from the Third Reform Act (1884-5) which allowed for a further extension of the vote and the creation of single-member constituencies, the session was dominated by the Irish problem. The Second Land Act finally delivered security of tenancy for Irish farmers but nevertheless the violence continued. In 1882 Lord Frederick Cavendish, the Irish Chief Secretary, was murdered in Phoenix Park, Dublin, by Fenians. Gladstone was now secretly coming to the view that the solution to the problem was Home Rule for Ireland, a view shared by Irish MPs led by Charles Stuart Parnell.

Gladstone fell from office in 1885 but then suddenly revealed publicly that he would indeed bring in Home Rule. He was restored to power with the support of Parnellites and formed his short-lived third administration. Unfortunately for Gladstone, his Home Rule Bill was defeated by 30 votes. He resigned immediately but the issue caused a massive split in the party, with many Liberals seeing Home Rule as a threat to the union and the empire.

In 1892 aged 82 Gladstone was able to form his fourth administration with only one mission in mind – Home Rule. He was half deaf and blind but with a supreme effort piloted the Bill through the Commons, only for it to be defeated in the Lords. He retired soon afterwards. If he had succeeded, the further suffering of the Irish people would surely have been avoided.

He died in May 1898 aged 88. He had been prime minister for 12 years and 126 days. He was one of the greatest.

45. THE PRIME MINISTER ENJOYED WALKING IN GERMANY WITH A FÜHRER

Gladstone had many pursuits outside his political life. He was a voracious reader and according to his diary he read at least 22,000 books in his lifetime. He had a library on his Hawarden estate containing 32,000 books and he often passed the time sorting and rearranging them.

Gladstone held very strong religious beliefs, read the Bible every day and had some rather serious works published during his lifetime. He developed a keen interest in the ancient Greek writer Homer and propounded the thesis that Homer was an early Christian. He wrote a work entitled *Homer and the Homeric Age*. It was not well received by the critics.

Another pastime was tree felling. These trees were not saplings but mighty ancient specimens with a considerable girth. To begin with he selected trees on his own estate for the chop, but as he was also a regular visitor to various noble lords' country piles he would happily get to work there, too. To set the record straight, he was also a keen tree planter in Hawarden.

Walking was another hobby of his and he thought nothing of going for 30- or 40-mile hikes, often in mountainous terrain. (What did he have for breakfast?) He sometimes went on visits to southern Germany and naturally would take advantage of the opportunity to go walking in the Bavarian Alps. On one occasion he passed by Hitler's future haunt in Berchtesgaden and commented in his diary that he enjoyed a 'beautiful river walk... with a Führer.' We assume he meant a guide.

46. ... AND INDULGED IN
SELF-FLAGELLATION

William Gladstone was a man who wore his religion on his sleeve and many of the decisions that he made in government were measured against moral considerations. As part of his deeply held convictions, he saw it as his mission in life to try to rescue 'fallen women'. Even when holding the highest office in the land he would scour the streets at night looking for prostitutes to 'reform'.

Gladstone even took these women home for meals with his wife, Catherine, who approved of his charitable activities. However, she cannot have known everything. Endowed with immense energies and what one might term an overpowering sex drive, he all too often succumbed to temptation. Racked with guilt and seeking atonement, he would afterwards flagellate himself. We know this as he would signify the action by a little symbol representing a whip in his diary.

Not long before his death Gladstone solemnly declared to his son, the Rev Stephen Gladstone, that he had indeed sinned, but he had never 'been guilty of the act which is known as that of infidelity to the marriage bed'. (This must have been a relief to all concerned.)

Many of Gladstone's friends and colleagues were aware of his nocturnal escapades and were fearful that it might lead to scandal, but nothing was ever revealed about his secret life until long after his death. In fact, we only know all of this as the result of the publication of his diaries in the 1960s.

47. LORD SALISBURY WAS A FOREIGN POLICY SPECIALIST

Robert Cecil, 3rd Marquess of Salisbury, served in office as Prime Minister for over thirteen years and formed three administrations. He was also the last peer to hold the top job. Interestingly, he had an impressive aristocratic heritage as the Cecils (father and son) had been spy masters for Queen Elizabeth I. Despite all this he has been largely neglected by historians. He should by rights be dubbed the third titan of the Victorian age alongside Gladstone and Disraeli, although this rarely occurs. Perhaps this is because he showed neither the passion of the former nor the flamboyance of the latter.

He was born in February 1830 and attended Eton and Oxford, although he didn't complete his university studies due to ill health. He was the second son of the 2nd Marquis and after marrying a judge's daughter had to make do with a small allowance. He was elected as a Tory MP in May 1853 but the demands of his family of eight children meant he had to supplement his meagre income by writing long, erudite articles for the magazine *Quarterly Review.* His specialisation soon became foreign policy.

During the 1860s his elder brother died, and this meant he now became Lord Cranborne and heir to his father's estate. In 1866 he got his first real government post as Secretary of State for India but nine months later resigned as he objected to the Second Reform Act and its extension of the vote. He also despised Disraeli, the Prime Minister. In 1868 after his father died, he became the 3rd Marquis of Salisbury and moved back into Hatfield House.

It was not until Disraeli's second administration (1874-80) that Salisbury began to achieve prominence and his abilities were recognised. Disraeli worked hard to persuade him to come back into government in his old post at the India Office. With the passing of time Salisbury radically changed his view of the Prime Minister he had once so heartily disliked and they almost became buddies.

In November 1876 a crisis was developing in the Balkans as a result of Turkish massacres in Bulgaria. Disraeli dispatched him on a mission to the Sultan in Constantinople where Salisbury met up with representatives of the Great Powers of Europe. The assembled dignitaries presented the Turkish leader with a list of demands which he subsequently rejected. However, it turned out to be a decisive moment in his career as Salisbury had shown himself to be an adroit diplomatist; although the mission was a failure, he returned a hero.

He was rewarded with the office of Foreign Secretary two years later. He did much of the groundwork for the Congress of Berlin (1878) and persuaded the Sultan to hand over Cyprus to Britain for use as a base. The Congress became the centre piece of Disraeli's administration which resulted in Russia being forced out of the Balkans.

Disraeli died in 1881 and Salisbury soon took over leadership of the party.

48. HE PRESIDED AT THE HEIGHT OF BRITAIN'S IMPERIAL MIGHT

The new leader dealt deftly with the first crisis to confront the party in 1884. Gladstone, well into his second administration, was intent on introducing a Third Reform Bill which would offer the vote to the working classes in the counties. Salisbury, never a fan of democracy, at first threatened to veto the Bill in the Lords but then offered a compromise. He craftily offered to let the Bill pass if Gladstone accepted a Redistribution Bill, which would create single member constituencies (scrapping the two-member ones) thereby benefiting the Tories. Gladstone rashly agreed.

In June 1885 Salisbury was able to form a short-lived minority government propped up by Irish MPs. When Gladstone declared his readiness to bring in Home Rule the Irish MPs switched their support to him, but the issue tore the Liberals apart. Liberal Unionists, as they became known, feared Home Rule would lead to the break-up of the empire and formed a separate grouping in Parliament. By July 1886 Salisbury led a majority government and adroitly enticed these Liberal dissenters into the Tory ranks. Even outspoken radicals like Joseph Chamberlain were welcomed into the fold. The Tory party also changed its name to the Conservative and Unionist Party to accommodate the new intake.

Lord Salisbury now dominated government until the end of the Victorian era. Although he was no believer in reform, two measures of note were introduced in his second administration (1886-92). The 1888 Local Government Act set up county councils while the 1891 Education Act established free education up to the age of 12. However, as might be expected his focus was on foreign policy and for the first 11 years of his time in office he was also his own foreign secretary.

During his second term (1895-1902) the 'Scramble for Africa' became increasingly heated. The powers of Europe were seizing colonies across the continent and Britain almost went to war with France in the Sudan over the Fashoda Incident

(1898). In the end a deal was agreed which gave Britain control of the Nile while France got West Africa. More serious was the conflict that erupted between Britain and the Boers (Dutch settlers) in South Africa. The ageing Salisbury failed to stop the war engineered by Chamberlain, his Colonial Secretary, and the long, costly struggle over three years cast a shadow over his final period in office (1899-1902).

A central plank of his foreign policy had been that Britain should steer clear of permanent alliances on the continent which, he feared, would drag his country into an 'unnecessary' war. His government gloried in the term 'splendid isolation'. His period in office saw the height of Britain's imperial splendour marked by Queen Victoria's Diamond Jubilee in 1897. Alas, the Boer War rather took the shine off things.

Lord Salisbury retired in July 1902 and died just over a year later. His was a time of jingoism and imperial glory but he remained a dead weight against reform.

49. LORD SALISBURY HAD HIS OWN LABORATORY

The 3rd Marquis of Salisbury nurtured a keen interest in science and in due course set up his own laboratory in Hatfield House. The latest inventions and discoveries fascinated him, and his was the very first private house in England to have both electricity and the telephone installed.

There were sometimes unfortunate teething problems with the new technology. The electric wires which crossed the floors of his lordship's house were subject to overheating and members of his household were often obliged to employ cushions to extinguish small fires. On one occasion tragedy struck when the cable supplying electricity was blown down. An unsuspecting servant lifted the cable that was lying in wet grass and thereby became the first person to die of electrocution.

Lord Salisbury had his own private train, which ran directly from Hatfield to London. After lunch he would take the train into King's Cross, and it would be held there until his return. Salisbury suffered from a cognitive disorder called prosopagnosia, which meant that very often he failed to recognise familiar faces. One day he found a gentleman already ensconced in his private carriage just as he was returning to Hatfield and assumed it was a visitor for his wife. Little was said during the journey and Salisbury even asked the man to accompany him home in his brougham. However, upon their arrival he realised a mistake had been made and rushed off to his study telling a footman that he 'had left a madman in the hall'!

50. LORD ROSEBERY WINS THE DERBY... TWICE!

Archibald Philip Primrose, 5th Earl of Rosebery, once said in his youth that he wanted to win the Derby, marry a rich heiress and be prime minister and remarkably, he managed all three. He possessed enormous wealth, a great intellect and was feted across the country as an excellent 'stump' speaker. Yet despite all this, his career is seen as a failure. This was undoubtedly due to his hyper-sensitivity to criticism, his petulance and his pride.

He was born in May 1847 and was heir to a rich estate. He attended Eton where his masters soon noted his impressive intellectual gifts – and his laziness. As one of them put it he 'liked the palm but not the dust'. At Oxford he was expected to graduate with a first but left in a huff when he was informed that one was not allowed to attend the university and keep a racehorse.

The young Archibald inherited his earldom aged just 20 and sat as a Whig in the House of Lords. He was a handsome and gifted speaker with a melodious voice and was seen very much as a future potential leader of the Liberal party. He soon added to his wealth by marrying the heiress to Baron Rothschild's estate in 1878.

His first post in government was Under-Secretary at the Home Office under Gladstone in 1880. In 1885 he became Foreign Secretary for just five months, was surprisingly successful and was lauded by Queen Victoria.

Until 1892 the Liberals were in opposition, but Rosebery remained busy. He set out his ideas for House of Lords reform through the appointment of life peers and in 1889 he was elected as the first chairman of London County Council where he made a name as a progressive municipal reformer.

When Gladstone won the election of 1892 Rosebery returned to the foreign office where he pursued a strong imperialist policy making him extremely popular across the country. When Gladstone resigned in March 1894 Queen Victoria immediately sent for Rosebery, ignoring the two other contenders, Sir William

Harcourt and John Morley. Under pressure Rosebery agreed to Harcourt's terms for effectively jointly sharing the premiership. This turned out to be a disaster as they did not get on and no programme was agreed. Harcourt, as Chancellor of the Exchequer, introduced graduated death duties for the rich, which infuriated Rosebery. His only consolation was that his horse 'Ladas II' won the Derby that year and the feat was repeated in the following year.

In April 1895 he had a severe attack of influenza which left him out of action for months. He was also suffering from acute insomnia and anxiety, which may have been due to fear of being mentioned in the Oscar Wilde trial at the time. There was a suspicion by some in Parliament that he was homosexual.

In June the whole government collectively resigned over a rather minor defeat. It had lasted one year and 109 days. He did not return to frontline politics afterwards. He died in May 1929.

51. ARTHUR BALFOUR WAS KNOWN AS 'PRETTY FANNY'

In many ways Arthur Balfour was similar to the last incumbent (above). Both were born with a 'silver spoon' to nibble, highly intelligent and had the world at their feet, but ultimately both proved to be failures when reaching the top job. However, while Lord Rosebery faded from the scene after his shambolic tenure as premier, Balfour continued to hold public office after leaving number 10 and has the accolade of having the longest career as a cabinet minister in British history (27 years).

Arthur James Balfour was born in July 1848 and, as the eldest son, was heir to the family's considerable estate. His father died while he was young, and his mother had to bring up eight children alone, but this did not prevent young Arthur from attending both Eton and Cambridge. His future looked bright as not only was he very clever, charming and witty, he was also rich and had excellent connections. His mother was sister to the future Prime Minister, Lord Salisbury. His admiring family and friends called him 'King Arthur' while others at university gave him the nickname 'Pretty Fanny' in reference to his somewhat girlish and bookish ways. He also had the air of a dilettante and throughout his life he was noted for a general sense of non-commitment, lethargy and aloofness. He was one of the few prime ministers never to marry. One female friend wrote a little poem which ended 'Playful little Arthur, he / cannot take things seriously.' Balfour was elected to Parliament as a Tory MP in 1874 but didn't speak for two years and he did very little apart from busy himself with his passion, which was philosophy. In 1879 he published a book entitled *A Defence of Philosophic Doubt.*

By 1885 he had proved himself as a good debater and his uncle, Lord Salisbury, appointed him President of the Local Government Board. Two years later, to much hilarity and disbelief, he was given the challenging post of Chief Secretary for Ireland. However, to almost everyone's surprise he acquitted himself well, using coercion ('Bloody Balfour') but also land reforms to ease discontent. His reward was promotion to Leader of the House of Commons in 1891, a position which he held until 1902. By now his uncle was elderly and ailing and Arthur was seen as his heir apparent.

When Balfour was appointed as his successor in July that year it was one of the few cases of nepotism in modern British history – from this came the expression 'Bob's your uncle'. It all looked promising. Not only did he command a large majority but the Liberal opposition was deeply divided. Unfortunately, events soon conspired against him. To begin with, the worthy 1902 Education Act was introduced, which reorganised the elementary and secondary education system and placed it under the control of local government. However, this success was overshadowed by the fierce opposition of non-conformists, which also helped to reunite the Liberals. On top of this an issue suddenly appeared which would tear Balfour's government asunder...

52. 'NOTHING MATTERS VERY MUCH' WAS A BALFOUR DECLARATION

Very soon, scandals and divisions began to erode the government's standing with the new premier seemingly unable to show decisive leadership. Joseph Chamberlain, the charismatic Colonial Secretary, raised the thorny issue of 'tariff reform'. He believed that free trade was no longer serving British interests and that a protective barrier should be placed around the empire. The problem was that free trade was a shibboleth for many members of the Conservative party and a dangerous rift soon developed. Balfour tried to find a middle way of 'retaliation' tariffs if and when required, but Chamberlain resigned in order to campaign nationally on the issue and the government remained dangerously split. The scandal of 'Chinese slavery' in South Africa further sullied the government's image.

Balfour impetuously resigned on 5 December 1905 in the mistaken belief that the 'divided' Liberals would be unable to form a coherent government, but the opposite was now the case. They had come together over the issues which had split the Tories and scored a landslide victory in January 1906. Balfour's administration had lasted three years and 145 days.

This, though, was not the end of his political career. He remained Conservative leader until 1912 when he resigned in disgust over the Tory peers' reluctance to face reality over House of Lords reform. The First World War saw him once again return to government with his appointment to the War Council in 1914, where his considered contributions were very much appreciated.

By May 1915 he was First Lord of the Admiralty in a coalition government and was made Foreign Secretary the following year. In 1917 he went to Washington and successfully completed the important mission of persuading the American government and Congress of the merits of prosecuting the war against Germany and her allies. In November of that year he issued the Balfour Declaration, which, in a letter to Baron

Rothschild, stated that the British government would support the 'establishment in Palestine of a national home for the Jewish people'. This ultimately resulted in the creation of the State of Israel. He had always been fascinated by the story of the Jewish people and in later life declared this to be 'the thing the most worthwhile'.

Balfour also acted as Prime Minister Lloyd George's deputy at the Versailles Conference in 1919, at which he was a proponent of leniency towards Germany and a supporter of the League of Nations (a prototype of the United Nations). In the 1920s he returned to government as Lord President of the Council where even in old age he was a valued colleague. He retired in 1929 and died a year later at the age of 81.

His ability to appreciate both sides of an argument had made him an excellent cabinet member. However, he had lacked the man management skills required as prime minister. His laid-back, philosophical approach can be summed up by his own observation, 'Nothing matters very much, and very few things matter very much at all.'

53. THE LABOUR PARTY COMES INTO BEING

The Labour Party came about as a result of the rise of the trade union movement and the spread of socialist thinking. The Trade Union Congress (TUC) had been created as far back as 1868 but as the century progressed many trade unionists were beginning to take a more proactive line inspired by socialist groups such as the Social Democratic Federation (SDF). By 1899 the TUC decided to push for working class representation in the House of Commons and formed the Labour Representation Committee (LRC) to fight the next election. It was a broad church composed of various socialist groups and trade unions but also included the Independent Labour Party (ILP), which had strong Christian leanings. This meant that the future Labour party was never entirely socialist.

Two candidates were elected in 1900 but in 1906 the first breakthrough came with the Lib-Lab Pact (a progressive alliance formed with the Liberals) when 29 LRC members were elected. The Labour Party was formally created the same year with Keir Hardie as its first leader. Ominously for the Liberals, 21 of their trade-union-sponsored MPs defected to the new Labour Party. However, it was not until 1918 when all men and women over 30 got the vote that the Labour Party came into its own and slowly overtook the Liberals to become one of the two big parties of government. In 1924 and 1929 there were two minority Labour governments under Ramsay MacDonald, but it wasn't until 1945 that Clement Attlee was able to form the first majority Labour government.

54. CAMPBELL-BANNERMAN WAS GENIAL AND IMPERTURBABLE

Sir Henry Campbell-Bannerman, or C-B as he was known, was a seemingly modest and unambitious man who rose to the top job when the Liberal party was looking for a safe pair of hands. He is somewhat forgotten by history although quiz buffs will know he was the first holder of the office to be officially titled 'Prime Minister'. His personal achievements were modest, but he presided over one of the strongest cabinets of the twentieth century.

Henry Campbell was born in November 1836 and was the son of a wealthy Scottish businessman. He was educated at Glasgow High School and studied at both Glasgow and Cambridge Universities. He later acquired the name Bannerman after an uncle insisted on this addition after bequeathing his estate to him.

In April 1868 he entered Parliament as a radical Liberal for the constituency of Stirling Burghs, which he represented for 40 years. He was considered a good MP being both amiable and showing strength of character, qualities which would hold him in good stead later in his career. C-B's first appointment was as Financial Secretary to the War Office in 1871, where he assisted Edward Cardwell in his major reforms of the armed forces. He achieved his first cabinet position in 1885 when he was appointed Secretary for War, a position which he also held in the Liberal government of 1892-5. Unfortunately, he was on the wrong end of a bogus scandal regarding cordite, which resulted in the collective resignation of the government.

Thereafter the Liberals found themselves in opposition for some time. By 1899 the two erstwhile leaders, Lord Rosebery and Sir William Harcourt, had shown themselves totally incapable of working together and had flounced out leaving the party rudderless. Thus it was that C-B was elected to steady the ship. Aged 62 and unwell, he was expected to be a short-term, transitional figure. However, he soon proved an excellent leader, seemingly not fazed by the splits in the party over the Boer War (1899-02). Later, the maladroit leadership of Tory premier Arthur Balfour became an asset for the Liberals and helped reunite them, thus allowing C-B to win a massive majority in the January 1906 election.

His stellar cabinet included three illustrious future prime ministers: H. H.Asquith, David Lloyd George and Winston Churchill. However, his premiership was to be plagued by his own ill health and that of his wife, whom he devotedly nursed until her death. Some important reforms were brought in such as the provision of free school meals in 1906 and the creation of a school inspectorate. However, perhaps C-B's greatest achievement was his insistence on a lenient peace deal for the defeated Boers in South Africa. He passed away in April 1908 before Asquith and Lloyd George could introduce the first elements of the welfare state. He was the last premier to die inside no. 10 Downing Street and his final words were 'This is not the end of me.' His premiership had lasted two years and 122 days.

Asquith said of him that he was 'calm, patient, persistent, indomitable'.

55. ASQUITH PIONEERED THE WELFARE STATE

H. H. Asquith was one of the finest peacetime prime ministers of the twentieth century. He was possessed of a mighty intellect and approached the problems which beset his administration with calmness, patience and lucidity. However, when the country found itself embroiled in a world war his laid-back style was less appreciated.

Henry Herbert Asquith was born in September 1852. His father died when he was eight and his upbringing and education was placed in the hands of relations. His Uncle John sent him to the City of London School where his potential was spotted early on, and he was one of only two pupils in the whole country to receive a classical scholarship to Oxford University. As might be expected he performed exceptionally well, getting a double first and also, as he enjoyed debate, becoming President of the Union.

After leaving university he turned to law as a means of supporting himself and was called to the Bar in 1876, although for quite a few years his practice yielded little in the way of serious money. Despite this he married a year later and soon had five offspring to support.

During the 1880s Asquith became a more active member of the Liberal Party and helped prepare some government legislation. His acumen was soon noted, and he was found a seat in Parliament in 1886. Immediately, his speeches were appreciated for their trenchant and authoritative style, and he was earmarked by some as a future leader. His law career improved as well and at just 37 he was admitted as a Queen's Counsel on £5000 a year.

His wife died of typhus in 1891 and he married Margot Tennant three years later. She was a witty and indiscreet society figure who led an extravagant lifestyle – which meant Asquith now had to work even harder.

In 1892 Gladstone formed his last administration and was so impressed with Asquith that he parachuted him into the position of Home Secretary. He soon showed he was up to the job by dealing with problems on the basis of 'firmness and good sense'. After Gladstone's retirement in 1894 the government soon fell apart under the inept leadership of Lord Rosebery. Asquith was virtually the only minister to leave office with any kind of kudos and by 1898 the opposition leadership was his for the asking. However, he waived the chance in order to continue working at the Bar.

In 1905 the Liberals returned to power and Asquith was appointed Chancellor of the Exchequer. He brought in some progressive policies such as differentiating between earned and unearned income for tax purposes and in his last budget in 1908 he made provision for the creation of old age pensions for the first time. Asquith and the party had by now thrown out the outdated Gladstonian belief that poverty was an individual problem. They embraced the belief, in a radical departure, that state intervention was required to help the conditions of the poor. This was New Liberalism in action.

56. AS PRIME MINISTER HE FACED FORMIDABLE CHALLENGES

Upon becoming premier in April 1908 Asquith was determined to continue the radical agenda that he had pursued as Chancellor. It was a golden opportunity as he had a huge majority from the landslide victory of 1906 and enjoyed the support of the fledgling Labour Party, as well as the Irish Nationalists.

His own Chancellor was now the equally radical David Lloyd George, who had the task of introducing what became known as 'The People's Budget', which would deliver old age pensions for the over 70s – but also eight of the new and hugely expensive dreadnought battleships. This was to be paid for by a 'surtax' on higher incomes as well as extra taxes on property. These new impositions were deemed unacceptable by the Tory peers in the House of Lords who vetoed the budget; as their lordships had never in modern times rejected a money bill, it created a constitutional crisis. Asquith immediately ordered a general election in January 1910 in order to obtain a mandate to override the Lords veto. The result was that the Liberals lost their super majority but hung on with the support of their allies and so the budget went through. A further election was required later in the year to achieve a further mandate to remove the Lords' veto entirely, allowing them henceforth only to delay legislation. This then paved the way for other important Bills to be passed such as the National Insurance Act (1911) for unemployment and sickness benefits, and the creation of labour exchanges (job centres).

Several problems now piled up in the years prior to the First World War. These included suffragette violence, dangerous trade union militancy and Home Rule for Ireland. The last problem came to the fore as the Irish Nationalists now held the balance of power and the Lords could no longer block Home Rule as they had done with Gladstone (44). The Conservative and Unionist Party bitterly contested it and gave full support to the Protestants in Northern Ireland, who so fiercely rejected any union with the Catholic south that massive civil unrest was threatened. Such an outcome was only temporarily avoided when the government accepted that the North would be exempt and would remain separate from a semi-independent Ireland. The Bill, however, never passed as the war intervened and so it remained unresolved...

Throughout this time Asquith despatched the business of government with remarkable efficiency. Generally, by midday he was free for his wife's luncheon parties, but in the afternoon he enjoyed reading or going out for drives in the countryside. His regular companion was Venetia Stanley who was less than half his age. How close they were is a moot point but over a five-year period he wrote her 600 letters and sometimes dashed them off to her during cabinet meetings.

Asquith suffered from a serious predilection for alcohol. To some of his friends he was known as 'Squiffy' and once in a committee meeting he was 'so drunk he was barely able to speak...'!

57. ASQUITH WAS KNOWN AS MR 'WAIT AND SEE'

When war broke out across Europe in August 1914, Asquith was at first averse to getting involved. Some of his fellow cabinet members were pacifist by nature and he feared a declaration of war in support of France and Russia would result in several resignations from the government. However, when Britain's involvement did come as a result of the Kaiser's army invading Belgium, only two resigned. Asquith did not now command a majority as he depended on the Labour Party and the Irish Nationalists to stay in power and so a national coalition should have been a consideration. However, he discounted this idea and soldiered on as before.

To begin with the war went well with the Allies managing to halt the German advance in the west. By May 1915 the scene had changed. A 'shell crisis' led to complaints in the *Times* newspaper that artillery shortages were hampering the war effort, while the Gallipoli campaign against the Turks was clearly turning into a disaster. As a result of these pressures Asquith at last agreed to form a coalition with the opposition Conservatives and Labour.

Unfortunately for Asquith, the new coalition did little to improve the country's fortunes or his own. He appeared increasingly lethargic and lacking in commitment, perhaps as a result of losing his son Raymond at the front and the fact that Venetia Stanley had left him to get married. Both of these were heavy blows. But what grated with his colleagues was his regular weekend parties where he would enjoy playing games of bridge and settling back into an alcoholic haze. His whole approach lacked drive and urgency when, every day, thousands of men were losing their lives. It didn't help that he was famous for the phrase 'wait and see', which had become his regular refrain prior to the war.

At the end of 1916, Lloyd George, now the dynamic War Minister, suggested that a small war council should be created which would include himself but exclude the Prime

Minister who, naturally, refused to support this idea. Lloyd George resigned over the issue but so did Asquith, in the mistaken belief that Lloyd George would not be able to form a government. However, he readily created a new coalition with the Conservatives. Asquith and his Liberal supporters refused to support the new government, which also included several Liberals. As a result, the party became badly divided with Asquith in opposition going into a long sulk.

This split continued after the war at a time when the electorate tripled to 21 million as a result of the Fourth Reform Act of 1918. In the election that year Asquith could only win 26 seats and although he and Lloyd George buried the hatchet, the 1924 election only yielded 40 Liberal seats, far behind the Labour Party.

Asquith resigned the leadership in 1926 and died two years later. He had been premier for eight years and 244 days. He had led the last Liberal government and must share responsibility for the demise of his party.

58. LLOYD GEORGE WAS THE WELSH WIZARD

Lloyd George was one of the greatest figures of the twentieth century but is also a highly controversial one. On the one hand, he was possessed of extraordinary energy and drive, which resulted in many important changes to British society and government. He was also a fixer who by using his charm and powers of persuasion brought about game-changing deals. On the other hand, he was deemed untrustworthy and unscrupulous by many, and this was particularly true of his behaviour with women.

He was born Dafydd George in January 1863 in Manchester. The family soon moved back to Wales but then his father died suddenly when Dafydd was only 18 months old. His mother's brother, Richard Lloyd, took in the family of three children and soon spotted the exceptional intelligence of his young nephew. Uncle Lloyd, as he was known, encouraged Dafydd over and above his brothers and he was the only one allowed to attach 'Lloyd' to his surname. Dafydd and his brother William qualified as solicitors and worked together in their own practice in Portmadoc. His brother was later to work long hours there to support his brother in his political career. Lloyd George made a name for himself as a radical lawyer by winning a series of local court cases on behalf of Nonconformists against the Anglican establishment, and it was on the back of this that he launched himself into a political career. When he married Margaret Owen in January 1888, he made it quite clear to her that a career in national politics would take priority in his life.

Lloyd George was elected as a Liberal MP in March 1890 despite allegations that he had fathered a child with a widow. For most of the next decade he busied himself with Welsh issues such as disestablishment of the Church in Wales and land reform. However, the advent of the Boer War in South Africa in 1899 propelled him into the public eye. The Liberal Party was split over the war with some supporting the Salisbury government and others, like Lloyd George, opposing it, who were dubbed the 'pro-Boers'. He saw it as morally wrong and naturally sided with the poor brave farmers there who reminded him of the folks back home. Feelings were running high at the time and when he addressed a meeting at Birmingham Town Hall, he had to escape a baying mob dressed as a policeman.

Afterwards, he gained support for his stand on the issue and became a standard bearer for the radical wing of the party. In 1905 the Liberals were returned to power and Lloyd George was handed the post of President of the Board of Trade. He acquitted himself well and worked tirelessly in the role, producing a raft of Bills and in 1907 used his skills as a conciliator to avert a national rail strike. The following year saw a turning point in his career...

59. HE WAS THE 'MAN WHO WON THE WAR'

When Asquith assumed the leadership of the Liberal government in April 1908 Lloyd George was appointed Chancellor of the Exchequer. He soon set to with great energy redrafting Asquith's own budget proposals to cover new massive naval expenditure as well as old age pensions. The 1909 'People's Budget' caused uproar in the Conservative-dominated House of Lords due to a sharp rise in death duties as well as the 20% levy on 'unearned increment' on developed land and they vetoed it. Famously Lloyd George tore into their lordships in a speech, referring to them as 'five hundred men, ordinary men chosen accidentally from among the unemployed'. Two elections followed in 1910, which both allowed the budget to pass and stripped the House of Lords of their veto powers (56).

Lloyd George's welfare masterpiece came in 1911 when he introduced the National Insurance Act, composed of two parts: unemployment and sickness benefits. Regarding the latter he had to use his vast charm along with some coercion to persuade the medical profession and insurance companies to back it. The unemployment section required employees, employers and the state to make contributions and was the basis for the welfare provisions of the Attlee government (1945-51).

Regrettably, in 1912 the Marconi scandal blew up in his face. Lloyd George had unwisely invested in the American Marconi Company prior to the British subsidiary receiving a large contract from the British government. He was accused of insider dealing but was later acquitted. However, there was a lingering feeling afterwards that he was somehow 'untrustworthy' and this would come to haunt him later.

In the ensuing terrifying conflict Lloyd George really showed his mettle. As war Chancellor he acted quickly to steady the markets and made some rousing patriotic speeches (although he carefully made sure his own sons avoided the front line). In the Asquith coalition formed in May 1915 he used his great energies and ideas in the new Ministry of Munitions to transform shell and machine gun production. He achieved this by employing women in vast factories managed by innovative businessmen, with the result that shell output shot up from 70,000 in that May to 1,125,660 by July 1916.

In December 1916, the demand for a more dynamic prosecution of the war resulted in the replacement of Prime Minister Asquith by Lloyd George at the head of a new coalition with the Conservatives. He immediately set about revolutionising how government functioned by creating a war cabinet of five with a secretariat which, for the first time, took minutes of agreed decisions and responsibilities. In addition, at the back of Downing Street a group of experts and advisers were housed in what became known as the 'garden suburb'.

To reduce losses at sea from enemy submarines he introduced the convoy system but was unable to stop the generals from causing the terrible slaughter at Passchendaele during 1917.

By November 1918 the war was won and undoubtedly his vigorous leadership had been instrumental in bringing about victory.

60. THE PRIME MINISTER WAS A 'DYNAMIC FORCE' WITHOUT A MORAL COMPASS

The December 1918 poll saw a dramatically expanded electorate due to the Fourth Reform Act. The Conservatives had wisely decided to stay in coalition with Lloyd George, but the electoral results made grim reading for all Liberals as the Tories swept in with 335 seats while those Liberals loyal to the coalition only won 133 seats. The official Asquith Liberals in opposition were reduced to a mere rump. All this meant that the Prime Minister was a 'prisoner' of his coalition partners, who could dispense with his services at any time. Worryingly, it was becoming clear that Labour was set to replace the Liberals as the second party of government.

Luckily for Lloyd George, the Conservative leaders were in awe of the Welsh Wizard and happily followed his lead for the moment. At the Versailles Conference in 1919, which delivered the peace terms to the defeated Germany, he sought moderation although he was unable to avoid the defeated enemy receiving punitive reparations. Prophetically, he foretold that a resentful Germany would seek revenge. At home, the war had crippled the British economy and unemployment soon rocketed to 23.4%. In 1922 the Geddes Axe introduced swingeing cuts to benefits. Where was the pre-war radical, many wondered?

The crowning achievement of his administration was solving 'the insoluble' Irish problem in 1921. By utilising some sharp negotiating tactics he managed to get both sides in the conflict, the Irish Republicans and the Ulster Unionists, to sign an agreement that left Ulster separated off from the new Irish State.

The Conservatives were no doubt pleased with the deal but heartily disapproved of his disreputable sale of honours (peerages and knighthoods) with the money being stashed away directly into his own private Lloyd George Fund. It whiffed of blatant corruption.

By 1922 the Tories had had enough of his leadership, especially after the Chanak incident when he had threatened to go to war with Turkey. In October at a meeting in the

Carlton Club, Stanley Baldwin, a future premier, convinced Conservative MPs that he was 'a dynamic force' that would destroy the Tory party. The coalition was dissolved, and Lloyd George was immediately obliged to resign. He never returned to office.

In 1926 he became leader of the reunited but disintegrating Liberal Party, which by 1931 had split three ways leaving his Independent Liberals with a grand total of four seats. He was created Earl Lloyd George of Dwyfor in 1945 and died in March that year. He had been premier for five years and 317 days.

He was a great statesman, but he was also a 'scoundrel'. While his wife stayed in Wales to nurse his constituency, he set himself up in London with his mistress and secretary, Frances Stevenson. He betrayed them both as he was a serial philanderer and, most shockingly, even bedded his own daughter-in-law (admittedly the marriage was over). In politics and in relationships he was not bound by moral convention.

61. BONAR LAW WAS THE 'UNKNOWN PRIME MINISTER'

Andrew Bonar Law is undoubtedly little known due to his short stint as premier. Indeed, it was the briefest tenure of the twentieth century at only 209 days. He was the first prime minister to be born abroad (Boris Johnson is the second) and the first Presbyterian.

He was born September in 1858 in New Brunswick, Canada. His father was a gloomy Northern Irish Presbyterian Minister. His mother died when he was only two, but a kindly aunt took him away to Scotland when he was 12. Although possessed of an exceptional memory he did not go to university but instead joined his uncles' merchant banking business and later made a fortune by going into partnership with a Glasgow iron trader.

Like his father, Bonar Law was rather austere, seemingly having few pleasures in life apart from playing chess, golf and tennis … and cigar smoking. Another interest was politics and at the age of 42 he decided to run for a seat in parliament.

He was elected as Tory MP for Glasgow in 1900 and within two years was offered the post of Parliamentary Secretary of the Board of Trade, in which role he proved highly competent. In 1911 Bonar Law speculatively threw his hat into the ring in a leadership election and unexpectedly won when the two main contenders withdrew.

He set out to prove himself by offering the strongest opposition to the Liberal government, which was perhaps the most bitter stand-off in British parliamentary history. The issue which most fired his visceral feelings was that of Ulster. Due to his family background, he identified with it closely and he almost crossed a line into advocating insurrection. In the end he accepted a Home Rule Bill which excluded Northern Ireland.

The advent of the First World War saw him transformed into a statesman as he now gave his full support to Asquith's wartime government and later joined the 1915 coalition as Colonial Secretary. In December 1916 his intervention was decisive in replacing Asquith with Lloyd George at the head of a new wartime coalition and he was rewarded with the post of Chancellor of the Exchequer, taking on a key role as the prime minister's chief advisor and counsellor. On a regular basis Lloyd George would wander through into number 11 to discuss the day's affairs.

Tragedy befell him during the war as he lost two sons, and this was added to the loss of his wife in 1909. These blows and the heavy workload affected his mental and physical wellbeing. However, he agreed to the removal of Lloyd George in October 1922 and led the first Tory government since 1905. He won the November election on the motto of 'tranquillity and stability' but fell ill with throat cancer (all those cigars?) and resigned in May 1923, dying five months later.

He performed sterling service for his country and the Conservative Party. At his funeral in Westminster Abbey Asquith unkindly observed that the 'Unknown Prime Minister' is to be laid next to the 'Unknown Soldier'.

62. STANLEY BALDWIN WAS A THOROUGHLY NICE MAN

During his time in public office in the inter-war years Stanley Baldwin was generally held up by MPs from all sides of Parliament as a very 'decent' person. A deeply religious man, he was seen as very patient, easy-going and clubbable. He also had a dreamy, romantic view of the English countryside, no doubt formed during his upbringing in Worcestershire. He served his party as leader for 14 years and is one of few premiers to serve for three terms but is unique in having served under three sovereigns (George V, Edward VIII, George VI).

He was born in August 1867 and educated at Harrow and Cambridge, although he only achieved a third-class degree. After graduating he entered his father's iron manufacturing business and 'forged' a career there for 20 years. During this time, he also worked as a local councillor and had six children.

In 1908 he took over his father's constituency and entered Parliament as Tory MP for Bewdley and so like Bonar Law (61) he entered politics after working for a considerable period in business. Prior to the Great War he was an almost silent backbencher but that soon changed. In 1916 Baldwin held a treasury post in the 1916 coalition government and in 1921 was promoted to the cabinet as President of the Board of Trade. He was viewed by all merely as a competent and agreeable colleague but suddenly came to the fore when he threw his weight behind moves to oust Lloyd George as premier. His eight-minute speech to Tory MPs at the Carlton Club in October 1922 sealed the deal and he was rewarded with the position of Chancellor of the Exchequer in Bonar Law's new government.

Upon the latter's unfortunate retirement in May 1923, Baldwin was elected as the least bad candidate, but he soon proved a unifying figure with his style in cabinet being one of team leader and mediator.

His first premiership was a short-lived affair. Baldwin had become convinced that the solution to high post-war unemployment was tariff protection for industry and decided to put the issue to the public. However, the January 1924 election saw his government rejected and a minority Labour government was installed. This too was short-lived, and Baldwin returned with a thumping majority in October.

His second administration (1924-9) is remembered for two events. Firstly, Chancellor Winston Churchill committed a momentous blunder by returning Britain to the Gold Standard, which badly affected British exports and partly led on to the second problem, the General Strike of 1926. Although Baldwin handled the strike well, the harsh Trade Disputes Act a year later left a bitter aftertaste for trade unionists. However, it was not all negative as during this period there was a further expansion of the welfare state and a massive house building programme. In addition, all women over 21 were given the vote in the Franchise Act of 1928.

Baldwin was confident he could win the 1929 election on the slogan 'Safety first'...

63. ... AND HAD A ROSY VIEW OF COUNTRY LIFE

Economic problems continued to feature in 1929, so unsurprisingly the Tories lost the election, and a minority Labour government was formed once again. Soon after this the Great Depression swept the world. The Labour government was badly divided over how to deal with the mushrooming economic crisis, so MacDonald invited Baldwin to form a national government with him. The Tory leader was at first reluctant but in August 1931 he eventually agreed and took up the lowly position of Lord President of the Council. In essence this became a Tory government with the Labour leader a mere figurehead. A snap election in November 1931 then handed the Conservatives a huge majority, leaving Labour decimated with only 13 members officially in MacDonald's administration. The National government lasted four years and took several measures to overcome the crisis, including ditching the wretched Gold Standard and implementing some draconian cost cutting measures.

In June 1935 MacDonald retired and to everyone's surprise George V decided to call on Baldwin to form his third administration. He then proceeded to give the Conservatives another overwhelming majority in the November elections with nearly 54% of the vote.

One reason for Baldwin's electoral success was that he exuded reassurance and benevolence. He used radio broadcasts similar in style to President Roosevelt's 'fireside chats'. 'Honest Stan' gave the impression that he understood the concerns of the man in the street and sometimes he would also wax lyrical about life in the English countryside. In one speech he described 'The sounds of England, the tinkle of hammer on anvil in the country smithy, the corncrake on a dewy morning, the sound of the scythe against the whetstone, and the sight of a plough team coming over the brow of a hill...'

It is easy to believe that he lived in a fantasy land and failed to recognise the burgeoning problem of the Fascist dictators.

The truth is that behind the scenes in 1934 he had already set in motion expansion of the RAF and a major rearmament programme was underway in his last term of office, but, admittedly, its implementation did lack the requisite urgency.

His last problem at home was the Abdication Crisis in 1937, which he dealt with very adroitly by persuading Edward VIII that giving up the crown was the only way forward.

He retired in May of that year. He died ten years later and was buried in Worcester cathedral. He had been Prime Minister for seven years and 82 days. He dominated the inter-war period but after leaving office he was vilified by many for supposedly failing to rearm Britain in time.

The PM loved travelling by train and often alone. One day a fellow passenger came over to him and declared that he recognised him from their days at Harrow. After some exchanges there was a pause in the conversation, before he tapped Baldwin on the knee and enquired, 'So tell me, Baldwin, what are you doing these days?'

64. RAMSAY MACDONALD'S ORIGINS WERE VERY HUMBLE

Ramsay MacDonald remains a highly controversial character with regard to the Labour movement. He was instrumental in its creation and yet he also nearly brought about its destruction. He had a meteoric rise from the poorest of backgrounds in Scotland to the highest office in the land and became Britain's first working class prime minister.

He was born in October 1866 to a servant girl in Lossiemouth on the Moray Firth. The father was a ploughman who subsequently disappeared, thereby leaving Ramsay as illegitimate. This remained a sensitive point for him throughout his life. However, as he grew up he had two advantages – a heady combination of great intelligence and good looks. He did well in his small local school but by 15 he was working out in the fields. He was recalled to act as a teacher, and he continued there for four years before heading out to Bristol, then London, where he found various unsatisfactory jobs. Eventually, he had a minor breakthrough working as a private secretary for an aspiring Liberal politician, which gave him a good regular salary. However, around this time he became interested in socialist organisations such as the radical SDF (the Social Democratic Federation) and the more moderate Fabian Society. By 1892 he was a paid lecturer for the latter and supplemented his salary by working as a journalist.

At around this time the Liberal Party had a scheme to get working-class candidates elected under their umbrella as Lib-Lab MPs. In 1894 MacDonald put himself forward for this in the constituency of Southampton, but the local party snobbishly turned him down. It was as a result of this rejection that he turned to the Independent Labour Party (ILP) and stood as their candidate once again in Southampton in the following year. He was unsuccessful but met his future wife Margaret who brought him some financial security, as well as a family.

By 1900 the Labour Representation Committee (LRC) was formed in order to get more working-class men elected as

MPs. It was a mixture of socialist organisations as well as trade unions and MacDonald was selected as its secretary. He worked tirelessly, mediating between radical groups such as the SDF, which wanted class warfare, and the other more moderate ones. A mere two candidates were elected in 1900, but the breakthrough came in the January 1906 election when they won 29 seats thanks to his pact with the Liberals: the Labour Party was born.

Prior to the First World War he busied himself with party organisation and in 1911 became chairman. He controversially gave his full support to the Liberal government but in return obtained important concessions for the Labour movement, including payment of MPs and legalisation concerning trade union funds.

In 1914, MacDonald took up an anti-war stance as he believed the conflict was a product of British foreign policy. He continually campaigned for peace but was punished in the 1918 election and lost his seat. The future looked uncertain...

65. MACDONALD BETRAYED HIS PARTY

MacDonald had always towered over his Labour colleagues as he cut an impressive figure with a highly effective speaking style. This being the case, upon his return to Parliament in 1922 he immediately took over leadership of the party once again. Things were looking up in general, due to a very strong performance in the election that year with 142 MPs returned and it was clear that Labour was already supplanting the Liberals.

Life became even rosier after Baldwin unwisely decided to call another election after a year. The Tories were reduced to 258 MPs with Labour a clear second behind them with 191 seats. The Liberals held the balance of power with 159 MPs and decided to put Labour into power as a test of their suitability for office. Ramsay MacDonald became Prime Minister of the first Labour government on 22 January 1924.

At the outset the government was popular, although there were few achievements. He did have a foreign policy success with the London agreement by which the French and Germans settled their differences over reparations, leading to the Dawes Plan in August. There were also increases in benefits for pensioners and workers, as well as a social housing building programme. In November the Liberals withdrew their support and the Conservatives swept back into office after another election. However, Labour had showed that it was moderate and fit to govern.

The Tories remained in power until 1929. The election that year catapulted Labour into first place with over 37% of the vote and 287 MPs, but once again MacDonald had to form a minority government. Almost immediately, the Great Depression struck, creating an 'economic blizzard' with unemployment soaring. By 1931 the government was unable to deal with the crisis, which had left a massive debt, and which demanded cuts to unemployment benefits. MacDonald resigned but the king insisted that he had a patriotic duty to stay on and head a National Government (with the Conservatives and Liberals) with a remit to carry out the painful policies so inimical to his own party. He agreed (was it vanity?) but only 13 Labour MPs supported him and almost immediately he was expelled by his party.

Worse was to come. Later in 1931, an election was held in which the Labour Party found itself in opposition to MacDonald's National Government and was reduced to a rump of 52 seats. His government took Britain off the Gold Standard and he duly presided over the dreaded reductions in benefits. It was soon clear that the ex-Labour leader was no more than a figurehead for the Tories and with the passing of time he fell into an embarrassing decline with little effective authority. He lost his seat in the 1935 election and he died in November 1937. He had been Prime Minister for six years and 289 days.

Despite his achievement of creating and establishing the Labour Party, he is seen as a traitor by many. Revelations regarding his very close relationship with the Marchioness of Londonderry have reinforced this view.

66. NEVILLE LIVED IN THE SHADOW OF HIS FATHER

Neville Chamberlain came from a family who dominated the politics of Birmingham in the late nineteenth and early twentieth centuries. Throughout his life he demonstrated great determination and attention to detail but also obstinacy and a refusal to change a policy when it was clearly failing. Although he is remembered for his poor judgement regarding Hitler, he was also a considerable reformer both in local and national government.

He was born in March 1869 in Birmingham and attended Rugby School and Mason's College before being apprenticed with a firm of chartered accountants. His father, Joseph, was an important radical politician in the city and had gone on to be a towering figure in national politics. Neville was in awe of his father, but their relations were very distant. He remained very close to his three younger sisters and to two of them, Ida and Hilda, he wrote on an almost weekly basis throughout his time in national politics.

Joe Chamberlain had determined from the outset that his son would go into business and when Neville was 22, he sent him to the Island of Andros in the Bahamas with a mission to make a success of growing sisal for rope fibre on a plantation there. Unfortunately, it was a hopeless venture as the soil was too poor and so was the quality of the finished product. Neville worked tirelessly for six years but it was all in vain and his father suffered a huge financial loss. His perseverance had been admirable, but he had obstinately refused to face facts for far too long.

To redeem himself he beavered away in local business and within a few years was a leading city businessman in the area of metal-making. Like his father, he also decided to go into Birmingham politics and in 1911 he was elected to the city council. He very soon established himself as an excellent administrator, came up with radical plans on the Town Planning Committee and set up the first municipal bank. By 1915 he had reached the giddy heights of Lord Mayor.

At the rather late age of 49 he decided to enter national politics and was duly elected as MP for Birmingham Ladywood in 1918. Neville showed a meticulous command of detail and was given several government posts in quick succession. As Health Minister in Baldwin's 1924-9 government, he became the star of the party as he brought forward a huge raft of bills which comprehensively reformed local government and swept away the old workhouses and the Poor Law boards. All sides of the House were impressed.

In 1931 he was promoted to the post of Chancellor of the Exchequer. The Great Depression was in full swing, so he brought in protectionist tariffs (once espoused by his father, see 52) ranging from 10 to 100% to support industry. By 1935 he had balanced the budget after making savage welfare cuts but ones which he was able to rescind. By 1937 he was Baldwin's clear successor...

67. THE PRIME MINISTER 'MISSED THE BUS'

Neville Chamberlain became premier in May 1937. At the age of 68 he was one of the oldest men to enter number 10 Downing Street for the first time. However, he had lost none of his reforming zeal as in the period 1937-8 he pushed through legislation that improved working conditions in factories, nationalised parts of the coal industry and introduced a law allowing all employees to have a week's paid holiday. In addition, his 1938 Housing Act set about accelerating slum clearance. However, his time in office became increasingly dominated by the threat of war.

As Chancellor, Chamberlain had already made provision for the expansion of the RAF in his 1934 budget but like so many at the time sought to avoid war at all costs and a repeat of the horrors of another world war. Sanctions had proven ineffective against the Italian leader, Benito Mussolini, so Chamberlain decided the best way would be to try to woo or appease the dictators by ceding to their 'just' demands. With regards to Germany, it would mean allowing adjustments to the Versailles Treaty of 1919, but always on the supposition that Hitler's aims were limited.

France, Britain's ally, rather reluctantly went along with this. So, when Hitler reclaimed the Rhineland (1936) and took over Austria (March 1938) there was no protest. The Nazi leader was so emboldened that he then demanded that the Sudetenland area in Czechoslovakia should be surrendered to the Reich as there was a majority German population living there. After some shuttle diplomacy the British and French prime ministers meekly acceded to Hitler's 'final' demand at Munich in October 1938. The shameful agreement left the Czechs defenceless, and it was surely the greatest betrayal in modern British foreign policy. Chamberlain proclaimed 'peace in our time', but his belief that the Nazi leader was trustworthy was soon laid bare when in March the following year the dictator dismantled the Czechoslovak state and occupied Prague. It could be claimed that Munich gave Britain time to prepare for war, but it could also be seen as a critical moment at which to stand up to Hitler.

When the Germans crossed the Polish frontier in September 1939 Britain declared war, but the Allies did little and for over six months settled back into the 'Phoney War' and awaited events. On 4 April 1940, Chamberlain made a fateful speech when he alleged that Hitler had 'certainly missed the bus'. Five days later Hitler's forces invaded Norway. The debacle that followed there was blamed on the lacklustre Prime Minister and Parliament forced his resignation on 10 May. Afterwards, he stayed on and loyally supported Churchill in the new government as Lord President of the Council, but in September he was obliged to retire due to cancer and died two months later. He had been premier for two years and 348 days.

In domestic affairs Chamberlain was highly competent but in foreign affairs, you could say, it was *he* who had 'missed the bus', as he lamentably failed to stand up to the Nazi leader at Munich.

68. WINSTON CHURCHILL STARTED OUT AS A REFORMING LIBERAL

It is no surprise that in various polls Winston Churchill has been voted the greatest Englishman. The length and achievements of his career were remarkable. He was a member of the House of Commons for nearly 64 years, had a ministerial career that stretched from 1906 to 1955 (with some gaps) and was Prime Minister for over eight and a half years. He will, of course, be remembered for his leadership during the Second World War during which his momentous speeches galvanised the British nation. However, he was also a prolific author, who wrote over thirty books and countless articles and was an accomplished artist.

He was born in November 1874 into the aristocratic Marlborough family. His father, Randolph Churchill, had a meteoric career reaching the heights of Chancellor of the Exchequer before suddenly falling from grace and dying at 45 from suspected syphilis. His mother was an American society beauty who ended up having three husbands and sharing her bed with countless lovers.

The young Winston failed to impress at Harrow but did better at Sandhurst where he graduated as a cavalry officer. Before going out to India he visited Cuba and became somewhat embroiled in the war of independence there. Once out in India (1896) he was soon noted as somebody who was rather brash, an attention-seeking medal hunter who could also be incredibly fearless (reckless?) in the face of danger. All this was exhibited on an expedition to the North-West frontier after which he wrote a book outlining the campaign. Afterwards in 1898 he joined General Kitchener's expedition in the Sudan where he took part in the last cavalry charge of the British army. His involvement in the Boer War in 1899-1900 propelled him into the public eye as he was taken prisoner by the Boers but then made a miraculous escape. As always, he penned a flurry of newspaper articles and books to accompany these exploits, which were required to finance his lifestyle.

On the back of his fame, he was elected as a Tory MP in 1900 at the age of just 25. However, within a few years he fell out with his party partly over the issue of free trade but also on the alleviation of poverty. He had read the Rowntree report, which set out the degree of deprivation in York at the time, and this drew him towards the Liberals and social policy. Or a cynic might say that he had an eye on which horse was most likely to win the next election race. In any case, in 1904 he crossed the House and joined the Liberal Party.

The Liberals did indeed win the election (in 1906) and Churchill was rewarded with the position of Under-Secretary for the Colonies, but two years later Asquith promoted him to the Board of Trade. Working hand-in-hand with Chancellor Lloyd George he now unexpectedly became a radical reforming Liberal by firstly creating Labour Exchanges (Job Centres) and then a national insurance scheme for the unemployed. But events soon moved him away from social reform...

69. CHURCHILL DONS 'ALL HIS WAR-PAINT'

In 1910 Asquith moved Churchill up into the Home Office where he became the youngest Home Secretary since Robert Peel (see fact 31) aged just 35. The pre-war period was marked by a series of rather serious strikes and one unfortunate one in South Wales left a stain on him then and thereafter. Following a miners' strike in the Rhonda and Aberdare valleys in November he felt obliged to send in troops to quell the disorder there. The death of a man in a fracas happened just before the army reinforcements arrived but Churchill was unfairly blamed. Soon after this he famously made an appearance at the police siege of terrorists in Sidney Street, London, and seemed to be personally directing operations. For Asquith this all smacked of rashness, so he switched him to the post of First Lord of the Admiralty where Churchill was much happier.

Preparing the navy for war was much more to his liking. He set to and brought in some important reforms including converting the whole fleet from coal to oil, which increased the speed of the battleships. He also insisted on significantly enlarging the number of the new Dreadnoughts. When the First World erupted in August 1914, he pre-emptively mobilised the fleet and was widely praised. Unlike his Liberal colleagues, he found the prospect of war exhilarating and Asquith half-mockingly commented that he had 'got on all his war-paint'. However, in 1915 his scheme for knocking Turkey out of the war by sending a fleet and troops to the Dardanelles proved a disaster. The army became hopelessly bogged down with resulting heavy losses. It was not all Winston's fault, but he got the blame and was demoted to Chancellor of the Duchy of Lancaster. His wife Clementine said later that she thought he would 'die of grief'.

As he found himself outside the war cabinet he resigned and spent over five months in the trenches in France. He commanded an infantry battalion and by all accounts was well liked by the men and officers. The adjutant, A. D. Gibb, later wrote that he was amazed that 'a creature of such energy, confidence, fearlessness, self-indulgence and eccentricity could exist'.

Churchill returned to London in May 1916 desperate to be at the centre of events. In December his old friend Lloyd George became Prime Minister, but it was not until July the following year that he was finally appointed Munitions Minister and he made a reasonable success of it. He kept the front well supplied with shells, guns and tanks and his reputation improved.

After the December 1918 election Churchill was switched to the post of War Minister. He soon headed into trouble again by seeking to overthrow the new communist government in Moscow through the mobilisation of the Allied Entente armies stationed in northern Russia. However, he badly misjudged the mood of the country, which had no appetite for further conflict and reinforced the view of him as a rash adventurer. It ended in costly failure...

70. ... BUT THEN FINDS HIMSELF IN THE WILDERNESS

Churchill's failed attempt to intervene in Russia against the nascent communist regime marked a move to the right, away from his previous incarnation as a radical Liberal. This was further underlined by his hard-line support for the brutal 'Black and Tans' in Ireland. Lloyd George felt his judgement had come into question and moved him to the position of Colonial Secretary in early 1921 where he was instrumental in setting up the Hashemite dynasty in Jordan. However, by October 1922 his saviour, Lloyd George, was ousted by his coalition Tories and in the ensuing election Churchill found himself out of government and without a seat.

He nevertheless remained undaunted. Over the next two years he slowly moved back into Conservative circles and made various stirring speeches about the threat of Socialism and the rising Labour Party. By October 1924 the metamorphosis was almost complete when he was elected for Epping not as a Tory but a 'Constitutionalist'. To the surprise of many, he was immediately given the prestigious post of Chancellor of the Exchequer by the Conservative Prime Minister Stanley Baldwin. In his first budget in 1925 he harked back to his Liberal days by including provisions for a widows' and orphans' pension insurance scheme. More controversially, he agreed, after much consultation, to restore the pound to the Gold Standard. This turned out to be a huge error as it had a devastating effect on British exports and, in particular, the coal industry. This led directly to the General Strike of 1926 during which Churchill wrote for his own paper called the *British Gazette*, in which he was fiercely critical of the strikers. Naturally, this did not go down well with the the working classes.

In 1929 the Conservatives and Churchill were out of office. He was to be outside of government for the next ten years. There were many reasons for this. Firstly, the prime ministers of the period preferred not to have such an irrepressible and dominating figure in their cabinets. Much of the problem lay with Churchill himself. He tended to take up extreme positions in opposition to mainstream ones of the time. For example, he became a staunch imperialist opposed to the Government of India Bill, which devolved limited powers. Only a few right-wing Tories agreed with him. Later on, he became a prominent supporter of Edward VIII even though it was clear to most in government that his desire to marry Wallis Simpson and keep the crown was untenable.

A further cause which kept Churchill out of power – but which ultimately got him back into office – was the threat from Nazi Germany. After 1937 he relentlessly opposed Chamberlain's policy of appeasement with Hitler and warned of the dangers. After the Munich Agreement of September 1938, he spoke to the House and correctly predicted that Hitler would soon overrun the rest of Czechoslovakia. By September 1939 appeasement had clearly failed and Churchill was needed in government once more.

71. WINSTON HAS HIS 'FINEST HOUR'

With the outbreak of war Churchill was appointed to his old post of First Lord of the Admiralty, which he had previously held at the start of the First World War. All went well until April 1940. The Norwegian campaign was Churchill's scheme to cut off Swedish iron ore, which was exported to Germany via the Norwegian port of Narvik. It ended badly as the Germans pre-empted the British attack leading to a humiliating retreat. In Parliament, however, the blame did not attach to Churchill but rather to the lacklustre Prime Minister, Neville Chamberlain, who agreed to step down after an electrifying debate. Winston was not the establishment favourite to succeed, but reluctantly and with no good alternative he was made premier on 10 May 1940. He led a coalition government of Conservative, Labour and Liberal members.

He was immediately faced with perhaps the most critical position for Britain in the war. A large British and French army was surrounded by German forces at Dunkirk but by a 'miracle', 338,000 were delivered to safety across the Channel. France soon fell and Britain, some felt, was facing the possibility of defeat. Weaker spirits in the war cabinet such as Lord Halifax thought Britain should sue for peace but Churchill in his own 'finest hour' faced them down and demanded that Britain 'fight on whatever the cost'.

Churchill galvanised Parliament and the British people with his oratory and displayed remarkable energy for a man of 65, sometimes working a 90-hour week and although his staff also had to work long unsocial hours, some claimed a 'feeling of being recharged'. Working as he did, it is little wonder that he suffered three bouts of pneumonia and a heart attack during his wartime premiership.

The country then survived two of the most challenging phases of the war. These were the Battle of Britain and the Blitz, when Britain was facing the Nazi onslaught virtually alone. During 1941 the USA and the Soviet Union joined the conflict and Britain was slowly reduced to the role of a junior partner. Churchill's 'Mediterranean strategy', which hinged on the belief that Italy was a 'soft underbelly', was soon found wanting and he was forced to accept a cross-Channel attack on Nazi-occupied France, which became reality in June 1944. By 1945 the USA and the USSR were the big two and the British premier could do little to stop the Soviet steamroller imposing communism across Eastern Europe.

In domestic policy, Churchill accepted the 1944 Education Act but baulked at the Beveridge Report that promised free health care for all. This no doubt contributed to his being defeated in the 1945 election. He returned to office in 1951 at the age of 76 and retired on 5 April 1955.

He had been prime minister for a total of eight years and 240 days and died in April 1955.

Churchill had many faults and there were failures. However, in its hour of need, he gave Britain the purpose and leadership it so desperately needed.

72. CHURCHILL WAS A MASTER OF THE PUT-DOWN

Winston Churchill had a strong love of the English language, which was not only on display in his speeches but also in his witty repartee and his caustic observations about those around him. Some are generally well-known but as this is a book about prime ministers it would seem apt to include the following.

On Balfour he commented, 'I thought he was a young man of promise; but it appears he is a young man of promises.' And, 'If you wanted nothing done, Arthur Balfour was the best man for the task. There was no equal to him.'

He had few words of kindness for Labour leader Ramsay MacDonald: 'We know that he has, more than any other man, the gift of compressing the largest amount of words into the smallest amount of thought.'

On Chamberlain and his appeasement policy he noted, 'He has a lust for peace.' And 'You were given the choice between war and dishonour. You chose dishonour and you will have war'.

He was particularly cruel about Clement Attlee, deputy prime minister in the Second World War and future Labour premier: 'A sheep in sheep's clothing ... He is a modest man and he has a lot to be modest about.' And 'An empty taxi arrived at 10 Downing Street, and when the door was opened Attlee got out.' (Churchill disowned this one at the time but everyone assumed it was his.)

And finally, on Bernard Montgomery who was Britain's leading general in the war and was insufferably conceited: 'In defeat, unbeatable: in victory, unbearable'.

73. CLEM ATTLEE WAS A SOCIAL WORKER

Clement Attlee emerged from a stable, middle-class background to lead perhaps the most revolutionary and reforming of all peacetime governments. Measures such as the creation of the welfare state and the National Health Service (NHS) transformed people's lives for ever and immeasurably improved the well-being of the British nation.

Attlee was born in January 1883 into a typically large family of eight children. His father was a successful City solicitor. Clement was a frail lad, short of stature, who home-tutored until the age of nine. He then went to Haileybury public school and from there on to Oxford University. He was clearly very able but was painfully shy in public. After graduating in 1904, he read for the Bar, passing the exams with some ease. All seemed set for a conventional legal career when one day in 1905 he had a Damascene moment. One evening with his brother, Tom, he went to work in a centre for deprived children in Stepney in East London. He was struck by the abject poverty and misery there and soon became completely involved in the project, living on the premises as a manager for 14 years.

Attlee quickly cast off any previous Tory beliefs and became a fervent socialist. He later cited a reason for this an encounter with a small, barefoot girl. She asked him where he was going to which Attlee replied that he was going home for tea. Her reply was 'Oh, I'm going home to see if there is any tea.' He was soon involved in the Fabian Society and the Independent Labour Party (ILP) and overcame his shyness to become a regular speaker.

When war broke out in August 1914, he decided against the pacifist stance of many socialists and joined up. Amazingly, he served throughout the whole war in such theatres as the Dardanelles, Mesopotamia and the Western front. Upon demobilisation in 1919 Major Attlee immediately entered Stepney local politics, rising to the positions of Mayor and Alderman within a few years.

By 1922 he had ventured into national politics and was elected as Labour MP for Limehouse and immediately became PPS for the party leader, Ramsay MacDonald. In 1923 he was a junior minister in the first Labour government and also in Labour's second government in 1930 and rose to Post-Master General. However, when MacDonald decided to form a national government with the Conservatives a year later, he refused to join, calling it a 'betrayal'.

In the general election that followed Labour was reduced to a rump of a mere 52 MPs. As MacDonald had been unceremoniously ousted from the Labour leadership, a new contest was held and Attlee was duly elected as deputy leader. Four years later he ascended to the Labour leadership. Between 1940 and 1945 Attlee worked alongside Winston Churchill in the War Cabinet and as his deputy co-ordinated domestic policy. The 1945 general election had an unexpected outcome...

74. ATTLEE HEADS A GREAT REFORMING ADMINISTRATION

The great wartime premier was greeted nearly everywhere with polite applause and most commentators expected the veteran politician to win the election. Attlee was much more subdued and his wife Vi ferried him to venues in the family Hillman saloon. He received rapturous receptions. Many remembered the terrible interwar years when unemployment had stalked the nation and how the Liberal/Conservative post-war promise of a 'home fit for heroes' had proved hollow. Labour offered a genuine change and so, to the surprise of many, they swept into power with a landslide majority of 146 seats.

Attlee and the 'big beasts' in his cabinet had had some time while working in the wartime administration to draw up plans for office. In addition, they had gained enormous experience of working within the machinery of government. The key players were Ernest Bevin (Foreign Secretary), Hugh Dalton (Chancellor of the Exchequer), Herbert Morrison (Leader of the House), Aneurin Bevan (Health Secretary) and Stafford Cripps (President of the Board of Trade).

It was a brilliant team and Attlee was an excellent cabinet manager. As Prime Minister he was determined to follow through on the promises made in the election despite post-war economic problems. The Beveridge Report of 1942 had outlined the creation of a welfare state that would offer support for Britain's citizens 'from the cradle to the grave' and this was soon implemented through the 1946 National Insurance Act, which extended Lloyd George's 1911 Act and made it universal while the National Health Service Act brought free health care to all.

Some of Britain's key industries were in dire need of renewal and investment and these were nationalised. They included the coal industry, gas, electricity and road and rail transport. The Bank of England, airlines and the iron and steel industry were also added. In total, 20% of the economy was taken into public ownership and from now on Britain would have a 'mixed economy' of public and private enterprise. The economy itself lurched into crisis during 1947 but by 1950 it was eventually restored through the American Marshall Plan and careful control on spending. On foreign policy Attlee personally intervened to bring about the end of the Raj and the creation of the new states of India and Pakistan in 1948.

The government had kept unemployment remarkably low and brought about massive change. This being the case, there was disappointment when in February 1950 Labour only scraped back into office with a wafer-thin majority of five seats. It seems continuing austerity and rationing had disillusioned some. A further election in 1951 gave the Conservatives a 17-seat majority. Attlee stayed on as leader until 1955 and died in October 1967. He had been Prime Minister for six years and 92 days.

Peter Hennessy summed up Attlee's achievement: '1950s Britain... compared to *any* previous decade was a kinder, gentler and far, far better place in which to be born, to grow up, to live, love, work and even to die.'

75. SIR ANTHONY EDEN WAS AN UNFORTUNATE PRINCE CHARMING

Anthony Eden was another who started life with a silver spoon in his mouth and later became a Golden Boy who moved effortlessly up through the political ranks. However, upon achieving the highest office he proceeded to produce one of the greatest foreign policy failures of modern times.

He was born in June 1897 and was the third son of Sir William Eden, 7th Baronet. The family house was the rather splendid Windlestone Hall in County Durham and the Edens had been prominent in the area since the eleventh century. He first of all attended Eton before surviving three years on the Western Front in the First World War and receiving the Military Cross. Afterwards, he went to study at Oxford where he achieved a First Class degree in Oriental Languages (Persian and Arabic). He toyed with the idea of entering the Diplomatic Service but instead decided to go into politics – for which he was ill-suited. He was first elected to Parliament aged 26 in 1923.

As Under-Secretary for Foreign Affairs, he was soon making his mark and by the age of just 38 (in 1935) he was appointed Foreign Secretary for the first time. He was a popular figure who possessed great charm as well as good looks. However, under his smooth exterior lurked a darker character of violent temper, vanity, obsessions and deep insecurities. Around this time he took to wearing a stiff homburg hat, which soon became his trademark.

Suddenly, in February 1938, he resigned his post over differences in policy with Chamberlain regarding Fascist Italy. However, in 1942 he was appointed Foreign Secretary once again and worked so well with Churchill that after the war he designated Eden as his heir apparent. When the Conservatives returned to power under Churchill in 1951, he once again received the stewardship of the Foreign Office and awaited with impatience his turn to succeed to the top job. Unfortunately, in 1953 he suffered a botched operation to remove two gallstones from which his health never fully recovered.

In April 1955, the ageing Churchill finally stepped down and Eden moved into No. 10. After calling an election which increased his majority, doubts began to emerge about his ability to govern. The event that scuppered his premiership was Suez. In July 1956, Abdul Nasser, the Egyptian leader, seized and nationalised the Suez Canal, which belonged to Britain and France. Suffering from persistent fevers and 'practically living on Benzedrine', Eden agreed to a hare-brained scheme whereby British and French troops would intervene and seize back the Canal after an Israeli attack on Egypt. Under American and UN pressure the Anglo-French forces were obliged to withdraw in humiliating fashion. Eden then misled Parliament by denying all knowledge of the scheme. It was perhaps Britain's greatest foreign policy disaster of the twentieth century and underlined her diminished position as a world power.

Upon doctor's advice he resigned in January 1957. He had been premier for one year and 279 days. He lived on for another 20 years and died in January 1977.

England, unlike junior nations,
Wears officers' long combinations,
So no embarrassment was felt
By the Church, the Government or the Crown.
But I saw the Thames like a grubby old belt
And England's trousers falling down.

Adrian Mitchell, 'Remember Suez?'

76. HAROLD MACMILLAN HAD A TROUBLED PRIVATE LIFE

Prior to the Second World War, Harold Macmillan was seen very much as an outsider whose progressive ideas kept him out of government. However, after the war he was transformed into an ambitious, power-hungry politician who promoted himself as a stalwart member of the grouse-shooting fraternity.

He was born in February 1894. The family had made their fortune from the Macmillan publishing company, founded in the previous century. He attended Eton but left early due to ill-health. Likewise, he did not complete his time at Oxford, this time due to the outbreak of war in 1914. He served on the Western Front from 1915-18, was wounded three times and was no doubt lucky to survive.

After the war he immersed himself in the publishing business as senior editor and had a rather enjoyable time meeting the various authors. However, by the age of 30 his mind had turned to politics and in 1924 he was elected to Parliament for the constituency of Stockton-On-Tees. He had been appalled by the plight of the unemployed and joined a progressive Tory group dubbed the YMCA, which looked at unorthodox economic measures as ways of getting people back to work. One of this group was the handsome and amusing MP Robert Boothby who was to have an unfortunate impact on Macmillan's private life.

In 1920 Macmillan had married Lady Dorothy Cavendish, daughter of the Duke of Devonshire. By all accounts she soon became bored by her unexciting husband and upon meeting Boothby immediately fell 'head over heels' in love. They started what was to become a lifelong affair that was pursued with minimum discretion. Allegedly, Macmillan's third daughter was Boothby's. Deeply hurt, Harold retreated into his books and politics.

During the 1930s he continued to espouse radical economic ideas. He was opposed to Chamberlain's policy of appeasement and voted for his dismissal in 1940. His ensuing inclusion in Churchill's coalition marked a huge turning point in his career. At 46 it was his first government appointment and new opportunities soon opened up. Two years later he was appointed as Resident Minister at the headquarters of the American commander Dwight Eisenhower who was stationed in North Africa at the time. He blossomed in his new role as liaison man and proved highly effective. His reward a year later was to be made Acting President of the Allied Control Commission attached to British General Harold Alexander in Italy. His remit also covered Yugoslavia and Greece, and he is credited with preventing a communist takeover in the latter.

In 1945 he returned a much more outgoing personality interested in achieving high office. In 1951 as Housing and Local Government Minister he was given the daunting task of building 300,000 houses – something which he achieved. In the period 1955-7 he was Foreign Secretary and then Chancellor of the Exchequer, but it was not his 'finest hour', as he misled Eden into believing that he would have American support over Suez. Eden resigned in January 1957...

77. MACMILLAN GOES FROM 'SUPERMAC' TO 'MAC THE KNIFE'

After the resignation of Eden, the two leading contenders for the mantle were Rab Butler and Macmillan. The matter was settled by two Lords, Lord Salisbury and Lord Kilmair, who interviewed each member of the cabinet in turn. The former had a speech impediment and every time he enquired, 'Well, which is it, Wab or Hawold?' In the end it was 'Hawold'.

Macmillan was 63 at the time of his accession and had the difficult task of rebuilding the party after the shenanigans of Suez. He dealt with various resignations and rebellions with equanimity and he developed a reputation for 'unflappability'.

Macmillan's image and his government were reminiscent of a bygone era. Typically, he was often pictured sporting Edwardian era clothes and enjoying grouse moor shooting. He appointed 35 old Etonians to his government, seven of whom were in the cabinet. However, he became something of a showman and a TV personality, and his popularity soared due to increasing affluence in the country. In July 1957 he came out with the famous phrase that the 'people have never had it so good' and when the cartoonist 'Vicky' mocked him with the epithet 'Supermac', it stuck and redounded to his benefit.

It was no surprise that the Conservatives won the 1959 election with an increased majority. Afterwards, however, matters began to sour. His application to join the EEC in 1961 was badly handled and subsequently rejected by the French President De Gaulle. In addition, economic problems resulted in a slump in his poll ratings. In July 1962 he decided to reinvigorate his government by abruptly sacking a third of his cabinet. This 'night of the long knives' was seen as panicky and eroded his 'unflappable' image. He was now dubbed 'Mac the Knife' instead.

After this, his premiership seemed to spiral downwards. Two events seemed to show that he had lost his touch. The Vassall spy scandal was soon followed by the Profumo Affair in 1963. In the latter, his War Minister was discovered to be having an affair with Christine Keeler who was also seeing a Soviet agent. Macmillan's government was shaken by the scandal and in a vote of confidence his support was seen to be ebbing away.

By now he was nearly 70 and many in the Tory party wanted him to make way for a younger man prior to the next election. Unfortunately for Macmillan, his firm decision to soldier on was pre-empted by an emergency prostate operation. He hastily decided to resign but immediately regretted it when informed that the cancer was benign. From his hospital bed he now engineered the succession, but instead of bequeathing the premiership to any of the frontrunners he chose an outsider, Alec Douglas-Home. The reason for this remains unclear but it was a gross disservice to his party.

He had been premier for six years and 281 days. In the end he was not a reformer and little was achieved during his tenure. He became Lord Stockton on his 90th birthday and died in December 1986.

78. SIR ALEC WAS BORN IN THE WRONG CENTURY

Sir Alec Douglas-Home (pronounced *Hume*) was an unlikely prime minister for the second half of the twentieth century. You would have to go back to 1902 and Lord Salisbury to find an aristocrat sitting in number 10. He was seemingly out of place for the modern age and was certainly not media savvy. He was the 14th prime minister of the century and also the 14th earl.

Alec Dunglass was born in July 1903 to an immensely wealthy Scottish family. His grandfather owned vast estates of 100,000 acres. He attended Eton and Oxford but was not given to academic excellence. Instead, he preferred a carefree existence devoted to cricket, racing, hunting and champagne. However, by the age of 28 his mind had turned to politics and was elected to Parliament in 1931. He was immediately given junior posts as Parliamentary Private Secretary (PPS) to various ministers and eventually ended up PPS to the Prime Minister, Neville Chamberlain, five years later. He remained loyally by his side until his political demise in 1940. The Second World War was not a good time for Alec. He caught spinal tuberculosis and after an operation had to spend two years on his back encased in plaster. (You could say he was thoroughly plastered!)

His father died in 1951 and he moved to the House of Lords as the 14th Earl of Home. He continued to move slowly up the ranks and by 1955 achieved his first cabinet post as Secretary of State for Commonwealth Relations. He stayed there for five years until 1960 when Macmillan catapulted him into the position of Foreign Secretary. It was seen as a strangely reckless act to give this prestige position to a peer and the *Daily Mirror* compared it to Caligula making his favourite horse a consul.

The second bizarre action by Macmillan was to promote Lord Home into the premiership after his own resignation. At first, Home had not seen himself as a contender but had then changed his mind. He was duly appointed Prime Minister in October 1963. His first act was to take advantage of a new law and disclaim his peerage and he now became Sir Alec Douglas-Home. Strangely, this left him without a seat in either house until November, when he was duly elected.

Throughout his tenure Sir Alec was entirely outclassed by the Labour leader, Harold Wilson. His skull-like features and patronising comments did not endear him to the electorate. In the general election that came a year later his one memorable witticism was to refer to his opponent as 'the 14th Mr Wilson'. Labour subsequently won with a tiny four-seat majority. Sir Alec had been Prime Minister for 362 days.

He stayed on as party chief and oversaw the creation of a modern electoral system for the Conservative leadership. He resigned in July 1965 but returned as Foreign Secretary from 1970 until 1974. Soon after, he was once more ennobled as Lord Home of the Hirsel. He died aged 92 in October 1995.

79. THE PRIME MINISTER ENJOYED FLOWER ARRANGING

Sir Alec Douglas-Home had various hobbies and interests, some more unusual than others. He enjoyed sports and learned to play cricket exceptionally well at Eton. He went on to play for various clubs and toured in South Africa with the MCC. Such was his prowess that allegedly he could easily have played for his country if he had so desired.

One interest was butterflies. On the very day war was declared, he and his brother Henry had gone down to the South Downs to search for a rare species. A special constable thought their behaviour rather suspicious and arrested them. Alec's claim that he was PPS to the Prime Minister was met with disbelief. 'Yes, and I'm the Queen of Sheba,' came the reply. A hurried phone call to 10 Downing Street ensured their release. Strangely, a very similar incident occurred a year later.

The oddest of his hobbies was flower-arranging. During his two-year confinement after his operation for spinal tuberculosis he became very adept at placing roses and tulips in a vase. It was something he practised for decades afterwards – 'because I was best at it, and if I didn't do it nobody else would anyway'. According to Rab Butler, his Foreign Secretary, as prime minister whenever there were periods of stress Sir Alec 'would go away on his own for half an hour and arrange a vast bowl of flowers'. This was perhaps an early example of mindfulness.

80. HAROLD WILSON HAD A METEORIC RISE

Harold Wilson is often neglected by modern devotees of the Labour movement which is no doubt due to the fact that his governments' achievements seem rather pallid by comparison with Attlee's post-war ones. And yet he was Prime Minister for nearly eight years, won four elections (the only leader since Gladstone to do so) and enacted a raft of measures which have transformed society to this day.

He was born in March 1916 in Huddersfield. His parents were lower middle class and the father was blessed with a remarkable memory, as was the son. Harold soon showed his abilities by getting a scholarship to the local grammar school and later won an Open Exhibition to Oxford University. Initially, his degree was History but after the first term he asked to switch to 'Modern Greats' (PPE). Permission was granted but only if he could learn German up to a required level over the Christmas break. In an astonishing testimony to his powers of memory he achieved this with ease. His performance at Oxford was stellar, achieving one of the highest First Class Honours ever awarded, as well as two essay prizes. Aged just 21, he then went on to become one of the youngest Oxford dons and lectured in economic history.

During the Second World War he worked alongside Beveridge on wartime economic planning. He was also employed in the Board of Trade where he focused on the future of the coal industry and wrote a book entitled *New Deal for Coal*. This then became the blueprint for the nationalisation of the industry after 1945.

In July 1945 Wilson was elected to Parliament as a Labour MP aged 29 and was immediately offered governmental posts. By September 1947 he had so impressed Attlee that he was awarded the position of President of the Board of Trade, marking him out as a high flyer and at 31 he was the youngest cabinet minister since 1806. In November the following year he achieved some fame for his 'bonfire' of wartime controls, but in early 1951 he resigned from the government along with

Nye Bevan, a standard bearer of the left in the party. The issue was the imposition of charges for false teeth and spectacles to help pay for the Korean War. Some saw this as an opportunistic manoeuvre.

In 1952 he was elected to the National Executive Committee of the party but within two years switched support from Bevan to Hugh Gaitskell on the right and became Shadow Chancellor after Bevan resigned the post. Gaitskell duly won the leadership and Wilson swore everlasting loyalty. However, in the leadership election of 1959 Wilson stood against Gaitskell but failed to win. Many in the party now saw him as a somewhat untrustworthy figure but Gaitskell felt compelled to retain him as his debating skills in the Commons made him indispensable.

In January 1963 Gaitskell unexpectedly died. Wilson won the subsequent leadership election after a run-off with George Brown...

81. WILSON THE ECONOMIST WAS STYMIED BY THE ECONOMY

Aged 48, Wilson contrasted sharply with the Tory leadership. Macmillan was nearly 70 and well past his sell-by date while his successor, Douglas-Home, was an out-of-touch aristocrat. Wilson came across as young and energetic but also classless. His previous divisiveness and disloyalty within the party were unknown to the public and he tried to foster an image of modernity by referring in his first party conference speech to the 'white heat of this revolution'. Prior to the October 1964 general election, Wilson avoided mistakes. He regularly trounced Sir Alec in the House of Commons and the opinion polls were favourable. In the event he managed to overturn a Tory 100-seat majority and squeezed into office with a four-seat advantage.

His immediate problems were economic for which, you would think, he was admirably prepared. The Conservatives had left the economy in a parlous state to which the obvious solution was devaluation. Instead, plagued by the notion that this would be a humiliation, he used the stop-gap measure of import surcharges. Despite this, the government was popular and Wilson proudly unfurled his National Plan for economic revival.

With a slim majority, a second election was soon in the offing and in March 1966 Labour secured a resounding victory gaining 97 seats. By April 1967 economic problems once more predominated with a run on the pound. Wilson again avoided devaluation and this time opted for austerity and abandonment of the much-vaunted National Plan. However, by November 1967 this proved to be insufficient and in humiliating fashion the Labour government had to finally accept devaluation. It was a bitter blow, which was followed by further deep cuts including the cancellation of the F-111 fighter aircraft.

Elsewhere, the Open University was established in 1969 and secondary education was radically reformed with the abolition of the 11-plus, alongside the setting up of comprehensive schools. In addition, the Home Office under Roy Jenkins brought in landmark legislation by decriminalising abortion and homosexuality. Wilson insisted on awarding the Beatles MBEs in the hope some of their popularity would rub off ... although John Lennon returned his.

In the 1970 election Labour suffered an unexpected defeat but Wilson returned with a minority government in February 1974 and then won a four-seat majority in the following October. At this time the Labour party was badly divided over the issue of EEC membership, which had been achieved under the Tory government of Edward Heath in 1973. He cleverly organised a national referendum on the issue in 1975 and allowed a free vote by his cabinet. The result was decisive for staying in and restored temporary harmony in the party. Wilson suddenly retired in March 1976 and gave the reason as wanting to give others a chance and the need for a fresh approach. In reality, he feared encroaching dementia.

He had been premier for seven years and 279 days and died in May 1995 aged 79. He had not been a great prime minister, but he had kept a fractious party united and had brought about important social and educational reforms.

82. EDWARD HEATH WAS KNOWN AS 'MR EUROPE'

Ted Heath came from relatively humble origins when compared to his Conservative predecessor, Sir Alec Douglas-Home. Indeed, his background bore a closer resemblance to that of his Labour rival, Harold Wilson. His time in office was generally marked by failure and bad luck with his one great success being that of securing Britain's entry into Europe. (He must be turning in his grave now.)

He was born in July 1916 in Broadstairs, Kent. His father was a carpenter and his mother was a lady's maid. Teddy, as he was known then, won a scholarship to the local grammar school, Chatham House, and then went on to Oxford to read PPE. He had a talent for music and won a college organ scholarship, which supplemented his meagre allowance. Politically ambitious, he was very involved with the university Conservative Association and was duly elected president of the Oxford Union. As an undergraduate he travelled widely around Europe and in Germany ended up at an SS cocktail party where he met Goering, Goebbels and Himmler, and which served to convince him of the Nazi threat. He graduated from Oxford in the summer of 1939.

During the Second World War he saw little real action. He served effectively in the Heavy Anti-Aircraft Artillery and finished up as a lieutenant-colonel. He was involved in the Normandy landings and in Germany after the war, and received an MBE. This experience had a lasting impact on him, and he was determined that such terrible wanton destruction should never be visited on Europe again.

After working in the civil service and a city bank he was elected as Conservative MP for Bexley in February 1950 and remained there for the next 51 years! He immediately went to work in the Whip's Office where he was seen as outstandingly efficient and rose to be Chief Whip in 1955. He held his first cabinet post as Minister for Labour in 1959 but a year later he was made Lord Privy Seal with a special remit to negotiate

Britain's entry into the European Economic Community (EEC), now the European Union. It was a plum appointment for him and he worked assiduously for 18 months, but it ended in disappointment when the French president, Charles De Gaulle, delivered his infamous 'non'. However, Heath gained kudos and was dubbed 'Mr Europe' by fellow Tory MPs.

In Douglas-Home's government he was appointed Secretary for Trade and Industry and after the Tory defeat in 1964 was Shadow Chancellor of the Exchequer. He was then elected as party leader in July 1965 due to his youth (49) and as a potentially good opponent for Harold Wilson. However, he was no match for his wily adversary and appeared wooden on TV. After the Tory election defeat in 1966 there were rumblings of discontent, but Heath managed to cling on to office.

He was much mocked in the media for his 'tortured and artificial vowel sounds' and 'insufferable upper-class accent' while impressionists had a field day with his forced laugh marked by heaving shoulders and flashing teeth.

83. 'HEAD TEETH' WAS AN UNLUCKY PRIME MINISTER

The June 1970 general election unexpectedly gave victory to Ted Heath with a 31-seat majority. The new prime minister had a list of priorities: the economy, Northern Ireland and entry into the EEC.

The problem of inflation, he had promised during the election campaign, could be solved 'at a stroke' by leaving it to market forces instead of a prices and incomes policy as practised by the previous Labour government. Unfortunately, the Chancellor of the Exchequer, Ian Macleod, passed away after Heath's first month of office, leaving a void as he was a trusted advisor. Nevertheless, at first Heath's economic policy appeared to work well, although the trade unions were hostile. His 1971 Industrial Relations Bill which sought to reduce industrial strife through the use of strike ballots was rejected by trade unionists, and in February 1972 the miners went on strike and were awarded a 27% increase.

Unsurprisingly, that same year inflation rose steadily and unemployment reached one million, so Heath decided on a U-turn by reinstating a statutory prices and incomes policy. Unluckily, in October 1973 the Yom Kippur war resulted in a quadrupling of oil prices, which drove a coach and horses through his whole economic policy.

In Northern Ireland he worked hard to achieve a power-sharing executive which included Protestants and Catholics under the Sunningdale Agreement but, unfortunately, this was torpedoed by the Protestant unionists. Only on Europe was he successful. He directly negotiated EEC entry with French President Pompidou and narrowly got it through the British Parliament. Even this has now been overturned.

By the end of 1973, the miners had put in another pay claim. Heath put the country on a three-day week to conserve oil and coal stocks and when the miners called a strike in February, he decided to hold an election on the theme of 'Who governs Britain?' Labour focused on the raging inflation, won more seats than the Conservatives and was able to form a minority government. Heath was unlucky as he had actually garnered more votes. He then failed to win back power in the October election and so now had lost three out of four elections. A leadership election became inevitable and in 1975 Margaret Thatcher ousted him, after which he went into the 'longest sulk in history'.

Ted Heath was a multi-talented premier. He became a skilled yachtsman winning the Sydney to Hobart race across the Tasman Sea as well as the Admiral's Cup race in 1971 (aboard his yacht *Morning Cloud II*). He was an expert musician and conducted the London Symphony Orchestra in the same year. He retired in 2001 and died in July 2005 aged 89. He had been premier for three years and 259 days.

As Tory leader Heath had some excellent attributes such as decisiveness and integrity, but he also had some serious failings. His style was authoritarian and brusque, and he often came across as aloof and lacking in human warmth. He was intellectually honest but a poor communicator.

84. JAMES CALLAGHAN WAS A TRADE UNION MAN

Callaghan grew up in hardship but overcame this to reach the top job. He worked his way up through the trade union movement and uniquely held all three great offices of state (Chancellor of the Exchequer, Home Secretary and Foreign Secretary) before assuming the premiership.

He was born in Portsmouth in March 1912 and was named Leonard James. His father suddenly died aged 44 thereby forcing the family into relative poverty. Len attended Portsmouth North Secondary School but left at 17 to work in the tax office. He soon became involved in his trade union and was assistant general secretary by the age of 24.

During the Second World War he served in the navy but generally had a quiet time. He was elected Labour MP for Cardiff South in 1945 and was immediately appointed to various junior posts in Attlee's post-war government. In 1951, Labour went into 13 years of opposition, but he worked assiduously to build up a formidable base of trade union support and this allowed him to obtain shadow portfolios, including that of Chancellor.

After Labour returned to office in 1964, Callaghan got the real Chancellor's post but had an unhappy time of it, as he was eventually forced to devalue the pound. Afterwards as Home Secretary (1967-70) he infuriated Wilson by openly opposing the 'In Place of Strife' proposal on trade union reform.

Upon Labour's return in 1974 he was made Foreign Secretary. He masterfully 'renegotiated' EEC membership and disguised the fact that the changes were mostly cosmetic. However, it enabled the government to get a resounding 'yes' vote in the referendum a year later.

Wilson resigned in April 1976 and Callaghan won the following leadership race becoming premier at 64. He was immediately popular having a reassuring air and oozing 'avuncular charm'. After a year Labour's tiny majority disappeared but he cleverly did a deal with the Liberals (the Lib-Lab Pact) to stay in office.

He managed to keep the economy on track with an IMF loan but his attempt to pin wage rises to 5% in 1978 ended disastrously. In the autumn he publicly dismissed the idea of an early election, which he might have won. He lived to regret it as the country was soon plunged into an avalanche of strikes which saw the dead remaining unburied and mountains of rubbish piled up in central London. It was dubbed the 'winter of discontent'. After returning from a summit in Guadeloupe, Callaghan tried to downplay the crisis in an airport interview. *The Sun* headlined it 'Crisis? What crisis?' and these words not uttered by him dogged him thereafter. In May 1979 he lost a parliamentary vote of no-confidence by 311-310, forcing him into a general election.

Distraught at betrayal by his trade union friends he put in an uninspired performance, losing the election to Margaret Thatcher. He had been Prime Minister for three years and 29 days. He died in March 2005 aged 93 making him the longest lived premier. He had preached party unity but had lacked strong convictions.

85. MARGARET THATCHER WAS NOT A 'CONSENSUS POLITICIAN'

Margaret Thatcher is arguably the most controversial of all the 55 prime ministers. This is undoubtedly a result of her belief in the righteousness of her policies and her utter determination to carry them through. Defeatism and compromise were words she viewed with contempt. She was, unlike many previous incumbents, a conviction politician. For some she was the greatest premier since Churchill but for others an uncaring power maniac. She was the longest serving prime minister of the twentieth century and the first one in 150 years to win three consecutive elections.

She was born in October 1925 in Grantham to a Wesleyan Methodist preacher and his wife. The father, Alfred Roberts, was a successful grocer and later rose to become mayor of the town. She learnt some important precepts from him which she carried with her throughout her life. He imbued in her that hard work and public service were virtuous and gave her a powerful moral sense.

At school she was indeed hard-working and diligent and won prizes for reciting poetry. In October 1943 she managed to get into Oxford to study chemistry and as a result later became the first premier with a science degree. She was already a fervent Tory and became president of the University Conservative Association. However, Margaret Roberts was not all work and politics at Oxford, as she set her sights on marrying the young and dashing Lord Craigmyle but was thwarted by the overbearing mother who thought a grocer's daughter unsuitable.

After her studies she worked as a research chemist in plastics but all the time she sought election to Parliament. Aged just 23 she was selected for Dartford but lost in both the 1950 and 1951 elections. The one consolation was that during her campaigning there she met her future husband Dennis Thatcher, a wealthy company director, who was to finance her future career.

She was now able to study for the Bar after which she qualified as a tax lawyer. Mrs Thatcher continued to search for a constituency but had to wait until 1959 before being elected as a Conservative MP for Finchley at the age of 33. Her views were distinctive as unlike her Tory colleagues she did not go along with the consensus view, which accepted the welfare state and the mixed economy. 'Socialism' and the Labour Party she equated with evil. However, she adroitly concealed her true opinions.

Within two years she was appointed Joint Secretary for Pensions and National Insurance and became the youngest woman minister in history. Thereafter she was handed a succession of shadow cabinet posts, the last one being Education. She was viewed as highly efficient and effective in debate – but perhaps a little too pushy.

After the Conservative victory in 1970 she became Education Secretary where she soon became deeply unpopular as a result of abolishing free school milk in primary schools due to treasury cuts. The cry went up 'Margaret Thatcher, milk snatcher'. However, surprisingly she did approve plans for more comprehensive schools than any other minister, Conservative or Labour.

86. THE PRIME MINISTER WAS SAVED BY A WAR

In 1974 Margaret Thatcher commented that she could not imagine a woman prime minister in her lifetime. Whether or not she was concealing her true ambitions, many would have agreed with her. So it came as a surprise when she threw her hat into the Conservative leadership race of 1975, considered more of a 'stalking horse' than a serious contender. Her campaign manager, Airey Neave, played a cunning game by making out she had much less support that she really had, thereby encouraging many more MPs to vote for her in the mistaken belief that she was unlikely to win. The ploy worked. She won the first ballot and romped home on the second.

As opposition leader she initially made a poor impression, although the Russians dubbed her the Iron Lady a year later after an anti-Soviet speech. In general, she came across as shrill and uncaring so her prototype spin doctor, Gordon Reece, set about changing her image. First of all he worked on her upper register, which he said was 'dangerous to passing sparrows', and hired a voice coach for her. He also softened her clothes and hair style.

The 'winter of discontent' of 1978-9 favoured the Conservatives and swung the next election in her favour. In May 1979 Margaret Thatcher became the first woman prime minister with a handsome 43-seat majority. Her administration was now going to be very different from past ones. Britain found herself in a deep recession but there was to be no repeat of Keynesian economics whereby the government would pump in more funds to provide a boost and reduce unemployment levels. Following the monetarist theories of the Chicago economist, Milton Friedman, she set about savagely reducing government spending in order to control inflation and reduce taxation. These deflationary policies together with high bank rates resulted in a massive fall in industrial output and a steep rise in unemployment. Many expected a U-turn but in the September 1980 party conference she reaffirmed her determination with the words, 'You turn if you want to. The lady's not for turning.' Those who opposed her in cabinet, the 'wets', were side-lined.

By the spring of 1982 she was deeply unpopular, and unemployment was nearing three million. Few expected her to win the next election but circumstance came to her assistance. The Argentinian leader General Galtieri decided that occupying the Falkland Islands would do wonders for his popularity. Reacting to this, Thatcher assembled a task force in three days and despatched it with the mission to regain the islands. Despite various setbacks and controversies, the re-conquest was eventually achieved leading to a massive surge of popularity for the government.

This marked a turning point in Thatcher's fortunes. Henceforth success mainly crowned her premiership (until the last year) and she became a 'virtual dictator' herself, believing in the righteousness of her convictions with decisions rarely receiving proper discussion in cabinet.

Exploiting her triumph, she decided to call an early election...

87. THE 'IRON LADY' TAKES ON THE MINERS

The result of the June 1983 election surprised no one. Labour was in total disarray with its moderate wing splitting off to form the SDP while Michael Foot, the Labour leader, offered a manifesto which lamentably failed to inspire voters. This, together with the Falklands factor, gave Mrs Thatcher a landslide victory with 397 seats.

With an enhanced majority Mrs Thatcher felt well able to deal with any threat from the restless miners. Arthur Scargill, the fiery coal miners' leader, was intent on taking on the Conservative government over its pit closure programme. Thatcher was determined to close down mines which were deemed no longer economic and Ian MacGregor, her hatchet man, was appointed head of the National Coal Board with a remit to carry out the task. He had already wielded his axe to the steel industry where he had halved the workforce and brought about several plant closures. Appointing MacGregor was a clear provocation and sparked the coal strike, but this time the miners would not be able to topple the Conservative government as they had done in 1974 as Thatcher carefully prepared for the battle by stockpiling and importing coal. Scargill called the strike in March 1984 but made a critical error by not holding a ballot, which undermined its legitimacy. Furthermore, not all miners supported the strike, as was the case in Nottinghamshire. A year later the miners were forced to give in and soon afterwards many of the pits were indeed closed down. The government had already passed labour relations legislation prior to 1985 which required trade unions to have strike ballots and reduced picketing with the result that in the following years both the number of strikes and trade union membership were substantially reduced.

After defeating 'the enemy within' Thatcher turned her sights on rolling back the state and 'reversing socialism'. She set about this by privatising the big nationalised corporations including gas, electricity, water and telephones. As a by-product of this enormous sell-off of state assets shareholder numbers grew from three to nine million and in total two-thirds of the public sector was sold off in this way. In addition, Thatcher had already pushed through her desire to create a great 'property-owning democracy' by allowing all council housing stock to be purchased by the tenants.

At the end of 1985, however, a crisis blew up which almost led to her removal from office. Defence Secretary Michael Heseltine wanted to stop the American company Sikorski taking over the British firm Westland. Her 'dirty tricks' against Heseltine led to the latter's resignation. Thatcher managed to survive an opposition censure motion after a poor performance by Neil Kinnock, the Labour leader.

In international affairs, Thatcher and the American president Ronald Reagan enjoyed a close personal relationship or 'love-in', both sharing the same ideological approach with regard to 'freedom' and the Soviet Union.

In 1987 she again called an early election and gained an impressive majority of 102 seats. Her policies on privatisation and council housing had proved popular and the economy was booming.

88. MRS T ENTERS HER 'GLORIANA PERIOD'

The result of winning three successive elections made Mrs Thatcher feel ever more invincible. She was becoming increasingly arrogant and just stopped listening. She told the world, much to the dismay of her cabinet colleagues, that she was 'going on and on'.

Ironically, she espoused freedom and 'taking government off people's backs' but her policies had the opposite effect. Through her reforms of local government and the health service there was a clear centralising impact. Her hatred of 'socialist'-controlled authorities led her to ruthlessly abolish the Greater London Council (in 1986), which was under the control of 'Red' Ken Livingstone, and other Metropolitan areas. In addition, powers were transferred away from elected education authorities and control of local government spending increasingly came under Whitehall.

The year 1989 saw her celebration of a decade in power. It was the longest uninterrupted period in office since Lord Liverpool (1812-27) and in retrospect it would have been a good moment to relinquish the premiership as from now on things began to take a downward turn. First of all, her ill-advised and obstinate pursuit of the Poll Tax resulted in massive unpopularity. Furthermore, her strident anti-Europeanism did not go down well with some of her cabinet colleagues.

The Community Charge or Poll Tax was brought in as a replacement for local government rates and was designed to curb expenditure by Labour-controlled authorities. It was trialled in Scotland in 1989 where it was unpopular and, despite this, was introduced in England and Wales in 1990. It sparked huge protests culminating in riots in central London.

Her cavalier handling of her cabinet added to her problems. Nigel Lawson, her Chancellor of the Exchequer, resigned in October 1989 over interference from her economic advisor, but there were already differences over his handling of the economy. There were also strong disagreements with Sir Geoffrey Howe who was demoted from the post of Foreign

Secretary to Leader of the House and who eventually resigned in November 1990 over her negative European attitude. In his electrifying resignation speech to the packed House of Commons he famously used a cricketing metaphor about how the 'opening batsmen' found 'their bats had been broken before the game by the team captain.'

This immediately sparked a leadership vote. Michael Heseltine put in a challenge and although he failed to win, he did sufficient damage to leave her four votes short of the required majority. Most of her cabinet now advised her, one by one, not to go forward to the second ballot. She later referred to this as 'treachery with a smile on its face'. However, she accepted their recommendation and resigned on 28 November 1990. She had been Prime Minister for 11 years and 209 days. 'It's a funny old world', she noted. She died in April 2013 aged 87.

For better or worse she was an effective leader who transformed the country. She is the only twentieth-century premier to have an 'ism' attached to her name – 'Thatcherism'.

89. JOHN MAJOR WAS THE 'GREY MAN' WITH AN UNUSUAL BACKGROUND

John Major may not have had the charisma of his predecessor or his successor (Tony Blair) but he did have some important successes and held office for six and a half years. Unfortunately, the image we have of his administration is coloured by Black Wednesday, internecine war over Europe and moral and financial 'sleaze' that permeated his parliamentary party.

He was born in Carshalton, Surrey, in March 1943. His father was nearing 64 and his mother was 38. His father had had a long theatrical career that included working as a trapeze artist. In later life he set up a business as a manufacturer of garden ornaments (including gnomes) which had prospered prior to the outbreak of the Second World War. When the business was restarted after 1945, demand for such products dwindled. Eventually, in 1955 'Major's Garden Ornaments' was disposed of, leaving the family destitute. The house was sold, and the five-member family moved into a very basic two-room flat which required them to share a cooker and the lavatory. There was no bathroom, so they had to wash in the sink or a tub.

Naturally, the young John was deeply affected. Although he had passed his 11-plus exam to enter the local grammar school he completely lacked motivation and left with only three 'O' levels. He had no career in mind and drifted between various jobs, but he retained an abiding interest in politics and so, aged 16, he joined Brixton Young Conservatives. In the meantime, he had struck up a relationship with an older divorcee who encouraged him to improve himself. Following this he secured a position with Standard Chartered Bank in 1965 and was posted to Nigeria, but a serious car accident there left him with a shattered knee and necessitated a long period of convalescence in the UK.

Afterwards he continued to work in the bank but alongside pursued his career in local politics and in 1968 aged 25 was elected to Lambeth Council, where he became chairman of the Housing Committee. His ambitions did not stop there, however, and in 1979 he was elected as Conservative MP for Huntingdonshire.

Initially, Major was not offered a government post but had to wait until 1983 to be given the lowly job of assistant whip. However, after an argument with the 'Iron Lady' he was surprisingly given a promotion and soon found himself Minister of State for Social Security. He was then offered the number two job in the treasury (Chief Secretary to the Treasury) under Nigel Lawson. Working long hours, he showed himself highly proficient in the task of negotiating spending limits with ministers.

Thatcher was impressed and he was clearly becoming her favourite. During 1989 he ascended to the heights of Foreign Secretary before being given the plum job of Chancellor of the Exchequer. However, he mistakenly persuaded Thatcher to join the ERM (Exchange Rate Mechanism) at too high a level for the pound, which would later come to overshadow his own government.

90. MAJOR WAS 'THATCHERISM WITH A HUMAN FACE'

In the 1990 leadership election he entered in the second round after Thatcher stepped down and clinched victory as her nominated successor. He became Prime Minister in November 1990 at the age of just 47, the youngest premier since Lord Rosebery a century before. Many saw his modest style as a breath of fresh air compared to his overbearing predecessor. He was certainly modest, as in his first cabinet meeting he wondered aloud whether he was up to the job.

One of the first tasks was to replace the Poll Tax with the Council Tax, which was achieved in double quick time by Michael Heseltine, Environment Secretary. The First Gulf War also redounded to Major's benefit at the beginning of 1991. Although he made positive noises about wanting to be at the 'heart of Europe', he skilfully negotiated opt outs on the euro and the Social Chapter at the Maastricht Summit in December 1991. However, the Eurosceptics in his party were bitterly opposed to his deal and the issue dominated his time in government.

In April 1992 he finally called a general election with a low expectation of winning in view of a continuing deep recession. However, Major's pleasant low-key style met with the voters' approval. In the event he secured an amazing 41.9% of the electorate and 14,093,000 votes, a figure which remains unbeaten to this day. But his majority was a disappointing 21 seats.

Almost immediately, events contrived to cast a long shadow over his administration. Black Wednesday (16 September 1992) was a disaster, the overvalued pound was forced out of the ERM despite billions being poured in to support it, thereby undermining the government's economic credibility. In 1993 he injudiciously embarked on a 'Back to Basics' campaign aimed at improving law and order and education. The press took it up as a moral crusade against Tory politicians and over the next few years a dozen Conservative MPs were forced to resign over sexual and financial scandals. 'Sleaze' soon irredeemably sullied the government's image. Few knew that the Prime Minister himself was not exempt, as he had had an extra-marital affair with fellow minister Edwina Currie for some time in the 1980s.

As a result of constant sniping at his leadership, especially from Eurosceptics, he suddenly announced his resignation in June 1995. He stood again asking his internal critics to 'put up or shut up'. In the end he was easily re-elected.

Major continued Thatcher's privatisation programme, selling off what was left of the coal industry, and the railways. He had success in Northern Ireland with a temporary negotiated ceasefire with the IRA, which laid the foundations for the Good Friday Agreement under Tony Blair. Major does not get the credit he is due for this achievement. By 1997 the economy was in excellent shape, leaving a golden legacy for his successor.

In the election that year his government suffered the worst defeat since 1906. People were tired of sleaze and Tory infighting. It was time for a change. He was a decent man who, arguably, had been over-promoted into the top job.

91. TONY BLAIR STARTED HIS POLITICAL LIFE AS 'BAMBI'

Tony Blair is very much the fallen idol. He was an exceptionally skilled political operator who had greater and longer lasting popularity than any previous prime minister. He was the first Labour leader to win three consecutive elections, two of them landslides. However, his fall from grace was rapid as a result of the Iraq War, with which he will forever be associated.

Anthony Charles Lynton Blair was born in May 1953. His father had been adopted, had been brought up in a council tenement block and had left school at 14. However, he studied hard in the evenings and ended up a law lecturer at Durham University and a barrister. He had ambitions to enter Parliament as a Tory MP and perhaps be prime minister but suffered a debilitating stroke.

The young Blair won a scholarship to Fettes School (the Scottish Eton) but did not enjoy the archaic system there, which included fagging. He was something of a rebel and narrowly escaped expulsion, but he was appreciated for his acting in school plays and got rave reviews in the school magazine. After leaving school he spent a gap year in London unsuccessfully trying to work as an impresario for rock bands.

He went on to Oxford to study law. He continued with his interest in rock music and was the lead singer for a short-lived student group called 'Ugly Rumours'. His movement towards politics came as a result of meeting the Australian Christian Socialist, Peter Thomson, and later the Scottish theologian and philosopher, John Macmurray. Through them he was converted to both Christianity and Socialism. Blair would later write a foreword to an anthology of Macmurray's work. Upon graduating he completed a one-year Bar course at Lincoln's Inn under the tutelage of Derry Irvine QC. Irvine had important connections with the Labour Party. It was there that he met his future wife, Cherie.

In 1983 he was elected as Labour MP for Sedgefield and in the House of Commons he found himself sharing a room with new fellow-MP Gordon Brown. Brown was much more experienced in the world of politics and the media and taught Blair a considerable amount about speech making and general communication skills. They became very close colleagues and shared a desire to modernise the party. Both Brown and Blair quickly moved up the party hierarchy and by July 1992, when John Smith was elected leader, Brown was Shadow Chancellor and Blair Shadow Home Secretary.

Blair proved highly successful in his new post utilising the phrase 'Tough on crime, tough on the causes of crime' and showed up very well in his TV appearances with his disarming smile and charm. In the party he became known as 'Bambi'.

Upon the untimely death of John Smith in May 1994, Blair was streets ahead in popularity over Brown. The latter reluctantly agreed in the 'Granita Pact' not to stand against Blair in the ensuing leadership election, which Blair then won easily. He now set about energetically implementing his modernisation programme...

92. NEW LABOUR ARRIVES IN GOVERNMENT

Tony Blair was determined to remould Labour into a centre social-democratic party and thereby make it more electable. 'Outdated policies and institutions' were to be rooted out. As he said, 'I was not born into the Labour Party,' which made it easier for him to bring in the reforms. One of the most important changes was to alter the wording of the contentious Clause Four, which had advocated nationalisation of all means of production. Blair's version excised the words 'public ownership'. The clause had been dear to many trade unionists and those on the left of the party, but Blair succeeded in getting majority support for the change, something previous leaders had tried and failed to do. New policy proposals brought forward were based on the work of 'focus groups', and the party was renamed New Labour. His popularity soared.

In the 1997 general election his party swept into office with a huge 179 majority. None of the new ministers had had any experience in government and it was immediately clear that this was not going to be the collegiate 'cabinet government' of John Major. Blair was intent on following a Thatcherite style with cabinet meetings being short and sharp. Instead, government would be dominated by himself and Gordon Brown as Chancellor and he would depend on three key advisers: Jonathan Powell, Peter Mandelson and Alistair Campbell. The latter two were his media 'spin doctors'.

This time there were going to be no economic problems such as had plagued previous Labour administrations. As Chancellor, Gordon Brown was able to splash the cash on the NHS and education.

Despite his enormous majority, Blair was not interested in radical change but instead focused on constitutional reforms. Scotland and Wales were offered devolved assemblies and the Greater London Council was reinstated. The Human Rights Convention was incorporated into English law in 1998 and the House of Lords was reduced to 92 hereditary peers (the rest being nominated) but disappointingly no further reform was achieved. Building on the progress made by his predecessor in Northern Ireland Blair was able to create lasting peace there through the Good Friday Agreement (April 1998) in which both Catholics and Protestants agreed to work together in a power-sharing executive. In some ways it was his finest moment in domestic politics as over three days he displayed formidable negotiating skills and stamina to seal the deal. Justifiably, he boasted that he could feel 'the hand of history' on his shoulders. On Europe he was to be disappointed as he was keen on Britain joining the euro but Brown thwarted him.

Blair's Christian faith influenced his foreign policy, where his interventions would be in moral defence of justice and democracy. In Kosovo (1999) he helped the Muslim population and was something of a hero there, with some locals naming their offspring 'Tonibler'! Two years later he became involved in Afghanistan. In June 2001 he called an early election...

93. THE FORAY INTO IRAQ BECAME A DISASTER

The 2001 election was very much a replay of 1997. Blair almost had celebrity status while the young Tory leader, William Hague, failed to make an impact with the electorate. Once again, New Labour was returned with a remarkable 165-seat majority.

The main focus of the new administration became foreign affairs. Blair had been very close to the Democrat President Bill Clinton and they had shared a centrist vision called the 'Third Way'. However, upon the election of the right-wing Republican President George W. Bush in 2000 he immediately cosied up to him despite their political differences. The 9/11 attack on America drew them closer and Blair afterwards pledged to Bush 'unconditional support' for the war on terror.

As mentioned previously, in 2001 American and British forces jointly invaded Afghanistan from whence the attack had come. This generally went well as Osama Bin Laden and Al Qaeda were chased off into the mountains. Bush now saw an opportunity to complete unfinished business from his father's time in office by invading Iraq and deposing the dictator Saddam Hussein, despite his having no connection with Al-Qaeda. Blair supported American aims but hoped it could be achieved under UN auspices. There was little justification for the invasion, but a case was made on the basis that Saddam harboured weapons of mass destruction (WMDs) which posed an 'imminent threat'. Unfortunately, UN inspectors in Iraq found nothing at all, but Blair still proclaimed that the Iraqi dictator was a danger to the world. A BBC journalist, Andrew Gilligan, claimed that the government was deliberately exaggerating the threat and many British people became convinced that Blair was lying (B.liar) culminating in huge demonstrations against the war. In a vote in Parliament 139 Labour MPs revolted but Conservatives MPs were persuaded and voted in support. The war and occupation of Iraq cost the lives of 179 British armed forces personnel and has left the country a cauldron of endless war and civil strife leading to perhaps 500,000 Iraqi deaths. Blair may have 'hoped for a Falklands but got a Suez'.

Meanwhile, Gordon Brown was becoming impatient. Blair, as part of the 'Granita Pact', had promised to leave office some time during a second administration but Blair claimed he needed to complete reforms on foundation hospitals and academy schools first. After some stormy meetings Blair eventually agreed to fight the May 2005 election in tandem with Brown with the proviso that he would step down before the following election. A diminished Blair won with a reduced 67-seat majority.

Eventually, he did relinquish office in May 2007 aged just 54. He had been premier for ten years and 56 days. Afterwards he secured the rather fruitless position of Middle East Peace Envoy but has also busied himself with various 'good causes' through his foundations. It is also alleged that he has since enriched himself to the tune of £100 million.

Despite his very creditable achievement of winning three consecutive elections, the dark shadow of Iraq continues to hang over him.

94. GORDON'S GIRLFRIEND WAS A PRINCESS

After a tour de force as Chancellor of the Exchequer under Tony Blair, many anticipated a signal performance as Prime Minister. In general, however, it was just another disappointing 'tail-end' premiership such as that of John Major after Margaret Thatcher or James Callaghan after Harold Wilson. The one bright spot was his brilliant handling of the financial crisis of 2008-9, which salvaged the international banking system.

Gordon Brown was born in Govan, Glasgow, in February 1951. His father was the Rev. John Ebenezer Brown and as 'son of the manse' Gordon had an austere, if middle class, upbringing. At school his star shone brightly. He excelled in all subjects and was outstanding at sports. Aged 10 he went to Kirkcaldy High School where he was placed into an 'E-Stream' for the brightest students with the result that he took his 'O' Levels at 14 and his Scottish 'highers' a year later. At 16 he went on to Edinburgh University to read History.

Unfortunately, he had suffered injury to both eyes while playing rugby at school and at university he was forced to lie down in a darkened room for six months. Alas, despite a new experimental procedure, only the sight in one eye was saved and a certain 'rigidity in muscles' on the left side of his face made it difficult to smile.

Nevertheless, he was a popular and very self-assured figure at university. He was elected as Rector against the principal's chosen heavyweight candidate and later took the authorities to court and won.

Even more surprising was that although he was a fervent member of the Labour Party his long-term girlfriend at the time was Princess Margarita of Romania. It was an unlikely pairing but true loved blossomed. She proved a useful ally when the authorities appealed to the University's Chancellor, the Duke of Edinburgh, to bar Brown from chairing meetings of the university Court. Little did they know that his princess girlfriend was the Duke's god-daughter, and that she was lobbying the Duke on Brown's behalf. Naturally, the university leadership's pleas fell on deaf ears. After five years together Brown and the princess went their separate ways. As she later explained, 'It was politics, politics, politics, and I needed nurturing.'

When it came to the final exams he achieved the highest marks on record. After university he lectured in politics for a while before working as a producer and journalist for Scottish television.

In 1983 he was elected to Parliament. He soon made an impression and teamed up with a certain up-and-coming MP, Tony Blair. By 1988 his popularity in the party was such that he topped the poll for the Shadow Cabinet and four years later was Shadow Chancellor. When Labour leader John Smith died in 1994, he expected to take over but under the 'Granita Pact' felt compelled to step aside for Blair. In recompense he would have complete control of economic policy in the event of a Labour victory at the next general election. Despite this, Brown felt he had been betrayed and retreated into himself.

95. 'NOT FLASH' GORDON SAVED THE WORLD

When Labour swept into power in 1997 Brown became Chancellor as agreed. At first, he kept to Tory spending limits, but he was intent on massively increasing spending on public services including the NHS. Partly to achieve this he placed 'windfall' taxes on the public utilities privatised by the previous Tory governments as well as £5 billion annually on pension funds. The latter had an unfortunate detrimental effect.

Throughout his chancellorship the economy continued to grow at an average 2.7% a year and this led him to make the regrettable boast that he had banished 'boom and bust'. This would come back to haunt him in 2008.

As co-leader of the government Brown also had a veto over large areas of government domestic policy. However, his feeling of bitterness towards Blair grew in intensity with the passing of the years. At times there was almost open enmity and this was reflected by the 'spin doctors' of the two sides who constantly briefed against the other's boss.

After the 2001 election Blair had verbally agreed in the Granita Pact (1994) that he would make way for Brown in the second term but instead delayed making any decision, which left Gordon in an increased state of bitterness and paranoia. It was not until the 2005 election that Blair agreed to a timetable whereby he would step down before the next election.

In June 2007, Gordon Brown at last became Prime Minister. However, he had lost some of his élan and appeared worn out by his grinding work as Chancellor and the years of waiting. Furthermore, surprisingly, he seemed to lack an agenda. However, all went well for the first few months with Brown dealing effectively with various crises and his poll ratings soared. A Labour billboard boasted, 'Not flash, just Gordon'. With such popularity he was tempted to go to the country in the autumn and allowed the speculation to run. After some dithering, he finally decided against it, which seriously damaged his standing. It became increasingly clear that not only was he unable to manage his image, but he was seriously disorganised inside Downing Street. Poor local election results led to questions about his leadership.

All this suddenly changed in the 2008-9 global financial crisis when he saved the world banking system from collapse. In September he bailed out three UK banks and the following month launched a recapitalisation of all British banks, all the while convincing French and German leaders to do the same. In April 2009 he hosted the G20 summit where he persuaded world leaders to inject $1 trillion in a massive rescue package. It was the defining moment of his premiership, and he went from 'zero to hero'.

Unfortunately, the old problems soon returned and in the May 2010 election an unpopular Brown was ousted. He had been Prime Minister for two years and 321 days. It seemed that power had come to him too late, and a tired, lumbering figure left the stage.

96. DAVID CAMERON HAD A PRIVILEGED BACKGROUND

David Cameron may have believed he was 'born to rule' in view of his privileged background. Indeed, his rise to power was seemingly irresistible and at 43 he was the youngest premier since Lord Liverpool in 1812. However, like Tony Blair, he will be forever remembered for one cardinal error – in his case, the Brexit referendum.

He was born in October 1966. His family home was a splendid Queen Anne mansion set in an idyllic village near Newbury in Berkshire. His father was a stockbroker who could trace his family lineage back to King William IV and his Irish mistress, and both parents' family histories abounded with Etonians, stockbrokers and Tory MPs. At the age of seven David was packed off to Heatherdown, perhaps the most exclusive preparatory school for boys at the time. Afterwards, of course, he went to Eton but became involved in a serious scandal when aged 16. Several fellow Etonians had been caught smoking and dealing in cannabis, but Cameron was fortunately let off as he had only been 'inhaling'. After this shock he knuckled down, got the required 'A' level grades, and went on to Oxford to read PPE. He did not show much interest in politics while there but is remembered for joining the Bullingdon Club famous for its excessive drinking and boorish behaviour. Despite this he left with a First.

Upon leaving university in 1988 he secured a position in Conservative Central Office. He soon impressed the powers there and within a short space of time was helping Prime Minister John Major prepare for PMQs and briefed him during the 1992 election campaign.

A few years later he met his wife, Samantha Sheffield, whose ancestry rivalled Dave's as it stretched back to Charles II and his mistress Nell Gwyn; she was also distantly related to Lady Diana.

Cameron was elected as MP for Witney in 2001. He came in as a moderniser and later dubbed himself the 'heir to Blair'.

By early 2005 he was already Shadow Education Secretary and with the election loss of that year he was poised to run for the Tory leadership. His speech at the Conservative Party Conference, delivered without notes, swept away the challenge of David Davis and in December he became leader.

He set out to 'detoxify' the party with such gimmicks as changing the party logo to a green oak tree and offering to 'hug a hoodie'. It partly worked as in the May 2010 general election the Conservatives emerged as the largest party but without an overall majority, so he persuaded the Liberal Democrats to join him in a coalition and became the 53rd Prime Minister.

The economic situation was dire so an 'austerity blitz' of cuts and severe spending limits clouded the next few years. In 2014 in the Scottish independence referendum the Scots narrowly opted to stay in the UK. The economy remained weak and the outcome of the 2015 election looked uncertain...

97. DAVE LOST HIS FINAL GAMBLE

An issue which had divided the Conservatives for decades was the European Union (EU). Euroscepticism was rife and even the Prime Minister was a strong critic of Europe. Cameron feared that the UK Independence Party (UKIP) led by Nigel Farage would wreak havoc in the next election as it could divide the Tory vote and allow Labour back in. Even two of his own backbenchers defected to UKIP. He headed off the danger by offering an in/out referendum on membership of the EU should his party win the next election. There was no doubt an element of hubris in this after winning the Scottish referendum, but this time the gap in the polls on Europe was narrower. In the end the Tories won the 2015 election with an overall majority of 12 after destroying the Liberal Democrats. UKIP had made little impact.

His plan now was to re-negotiate terms with the Europeans and then ask the people to decide. His renegotiations with EU leaders were disappointing particularly on the key area of immigration, but nevertheless he decided to go ahead with the vote.

In September 2016 he launched what was to become a highly divisive campaign. Cameron led the Remain side but Tory heavyweights such as Michael Gove and Boris Johnson jumped ship and opted for Leave. This undoubtedly proved decisive and this together with Cameron's own lacklustre performance resulted in a 52%-48% victory for the Brexiteers.

He immediately resigned. He had been Prime Minister for six years and 62 days. He left Britain divided, weaker and poorer.

98. THERESA MAY WAS GUIDED BY DUTY

It was said by many that Mrs May did not appear to take pleasure in holding the highest office in the land despite having craved it for so long. Perhaps this was because public service and duty was uppermost in her mind rather than enjoyment of power. It could also have been because the task of delivering Brexit dominated her period in office, a problem which in the end proved frustratingly intractable.

Theresa May was born in Eastbourne, Sussex in October 1956. Her father was a Church of England clergyman who no doubt instilled in her ideas of duty. Initially she went to St Juliana's Convent School for Girls but at the age of 13 won a place to her local grammar school. After this she went to Oxford where she declared her intention of becoming Britain's first female prime minister and was rather miffed when Mrs Thatcher got there before her.

She was elected as MP for Maidenhead in 1997. Very soon thereafter she had various shadow cabinet roles ending up as Shadow Secretary of State for Work and Pensions.

When the Tories returned to office in 2010 there was surprise when May was appointed Home Secretary, a post she was to hold for over six years. In this role she is remembered for substantially reducing police numbers and a failure to bring immigration down below 100,000. In fact, immigration grew substantially from both EU and non-EU countries. However, she did manage to deport radical cleric Abu Qatada.

Despite having been a Remainer in the EU referendum campaign she was elected leader of the party and Prime Minister in July 2016. Unfortunately, from the start she mishandled negotiations with Europe by making the statement early on that 'Brexit means Brexit', denying herself much-needed flexibility in negotiations.

The opinion polls gave her a huge 21-point lead over the Labour leader, Jeremy Corbyn, so she decided to call a snap election in June 2017 citing a need for an increased majority 'to strengthen her hands in negotiations'. In the event it turned into something of a disaster as May proved a poor campaigner. She frightened traditional Tory voters with a 'dementia tax' and instead of her promise to be 'strong and stable' she came across as weak and wobbly. She lost her overall majority but was able to stay in government with a confidence-and-supply agreement with the DUP.

Her position was now seriously weakened. Despite her stamina and dedication, she was unable to come up with a Brexit deal which suited the majority of Remainers or the Brexiteers. Over the next two years she suffered no fewer than 28 government defeats and 35 ministerial resignations. By July 2019 it was clear that despite her best efforts she would be unable to deliver Brexit and under pressure from her party she agreed to step down. She had been Prime Minister for three years and eleven days.

Although May had an incredible work ethic, she had lacked the leadership and media skills to make a success of her administration.

99. A PRIME MINISTER WITHOUT SCRUPLE

Boris Johnson is the most unlikely of Prime Ministers. From a young age he had an unswerving belief in his destiny but without a clear idea of what he would like to achieve as premier. Scruffy and clownish in appearance he is unconventional in both his private and public life. In addition, while some politicians are economical with the truth, he has developed lying into a science. Nevertheless, despite all his shortcomings he has a populist appeal among the electorate which has enabled him to achieve the highest office.

He was born in New York City in June 1964 and his full name is Alexander Boris de Pfeffel Johnson. The de Pfeffels can trace their ancestry back to George II and he has Turkish, German, French, Muslim and Jewish antecedents. His childhood was somewhat nomadic as his family was constantly shunted between America, the UK and finally Brussels where his father, Stanley, worked for the European Union (EU).

At Eton he was upbraided by his teachers for his 'idleness, complacency and lateness', although he did win prizes in Classics and English. At Oxford, like his fellow Etonian David Cameron, he was a member of the notorious Bullingdon Club but also became President of the Oxford Union.

After leaving university he decided on a career in journalism, although all time harbouring political ambitions. He started with *The Times* but was sacked for inventing a quotation. Afterwards he was Brussels columnist for *The Daily Telegraph* where he became adept at creating 'euromyths', for example, that eurocrats wanted to regulate the curve on bananas. He later became editor of *The Spectator* magazine in 1999 on the promise that he had no parliamentary ambitions. He did stand for Parliament but was allowed to write for the magazine and work as an MP. Conrad Black, the owner of the magazine, later described him as 'a fox disguised as a teddy bear'.

In 2004 Tory leader Michael Howard sacked him from his shadow cabinet position after it was revealed that he had lied to him about his relationship with a fellow *Spectator* columnist.

Johnson is a serial philanderer and has had three marriages and (probably) seven children.

By now he was a political celebrity and in 2008 he won the election for Mayor of London. Unsure of how to proceed, he relied on a team of deputy mayors and advisors to feed him ideas such as the Boris bikes. He was elected again in 2012 and in the same year he inaugurated the Olympic Games where he was amusingly left hanging on a zip wire. Such buffoonery did him no harm and even added to his popularity.

He returned as an MP in 2015 and a year later decided to back the Leave side in the Brexit referendum. Famously, his battle bus misled voters by claiming that leaving the EU would mean £350 million a week for the NHS. Victory in the referendum furthered his career...

100. A DISCREDITED PREMIER IS FORCED FROM OFFICE

To his own and everybody's disbelief Johnson was offered the position of Foreign Secretary by Theresa May in 2016 and his two years in the job were peppered with gaffes. Highlights were writing an offensive poem about Turkey's leader before later visiting the country and, most seriously of all, mistakenly stating that Nazanin Zaghari-Radcliffe, a British-Iranian woman imprisoned in Iran, was 'simply teaching people journalism', thereby causing her further hardship.

In 2018 he resigned over Mrs May's Brexit negotiations but upon her departure he was elected Conservative leader and Prime Minister in July 2019. Amazingly, Johnson was able to get a renegotiated Brexit deal which he then put before the British people in a December election. His chief adviser Dominic Cummings coined the winning slogan of 'Get Brexit Done' and huge swathes of Labour heartlands came out to 'vote for Boris', giving him an 80-seat majority. Britain then formally left the EU on 31 January 2020.

Celebrations did not last long as Britain was soon struck by the Covid-19 pandemic. Initially, he was cavalier about the impending crisis but he caught the virus himself and for a while was seriously ill in hospital. The only bright spot of his government's fight against this wretched disease was the rapid rollout of the vaccine. By the beginning of 2022 his administration was rocked by revelations of illegal Downing Street parties during lockdowns (for which he was later fined!) and scandals concerning the awarding of PPE (personal protective equipment) contracts.

His continued lack of judgement along with the usual denials and evasions led to mass resignations and an exasperated cabinet demanding he step down. He had officially been prime minister for two years and 348 days.